'This book is superb and it should be essential reading for anyone in fundraising... *The Porcupine Principle is* not a dry read. It is teeming with theories and ideas, and is a relevant and well-written challenge to all fundraisers.'
Lindsay Boswell, former CEO Institute of Fundraising and former CEO, FareShare

'Thoroughly enjoyable and thought-provoking read. This gem shares nuggets of wisdom through engaging short stories that will resonate with every fundraiser at every level of their careers. It won't just entertain you – it will leave you thinking!'
Katie Docherty, CEO, Chartered Institute of Fundraising

'Contains a wealth of ideas from someone who has been there and done it.'
Sir Stuart Etherington, former CEO, NCVO

'It is rare to read a book about fundraising that makes you smile, teaches you something unexpected and leaves you with plenty to mull over. Jonathan breaks down many fundraising myths with great humility and reminds us why we choose the rollercoaster of a career in fundraising.'
Judi Newman, CEO, St Elizabeth Hospice

'This is a great little witty read that is so well written. Best of all, it is probably the only fundraising book that might trigger a snigger. It's packed with wise fundraising vignettes and no-nonsense nuggets of myth-busting practical advice. It has great humanity running through it, and you will learn much more than just about fundraising. Enjoy!'
Sam Rider, NFP Catalyst Consulting

'Broken into bite-sized chapters and with references ranging from Take That to the Romans, to (of course) porcupines, this book is an accessible and engaging read. Its many practical tips made me rethink not just how I approach fundraising but also how I think about charities more broadly.'
Sarah Vibert, CEO, NCVO

THE PORCUPINE PRINCIPLE

AND OTHER FUNDRAISING SECRETS

dsc
directory of social change

Jonathan de Bernhardt Wood

2ND EDITION

Published by the Directory of Social Change (Registered Charity no. 800517 in England and Wales)

Registered address: Directory of Social Change, First Floor, 10 Queen Street Place, London EC4R 1BE

Tel: 020 4526 5995

Visit www.dsc.org.uk to find out more about our books, subscription funding website and training events. You can also sign up for e-newsletters so that you're always the first to hear about what's new.

The publisher welcomes suggestions and comments that will help to inform and improve future versions of this and all of our titles. Please give us your feedback by emailing publications@dsc.org.uk.

It should be understood that this publication is intended for guidance only and is not a substitute for professional advice. No responsibility for loss occasioned as a result of any person acting or refraining from acting can be accepted by the author or publisher.

First published 2007
Second print and digital editions 2024

Copyright © Directory of Social Change 2007, 2024

All rights reserved. No part of the printed version of this book may be stored in a retrieval system or reproduced in any form whatsoever without prior permission in writing from the publisher. This book is sold subject to the condition that it shall not, by way of trade or otherwise, be lent, re-sold, hired out or otherwise circulated without the publisher's prior permission in any form of binding or cover other than that in which it is published, and without a similar condition including this condition being imposed on the subsequent purchaser.

The digital version of this publication may only be stored in a retrieval system for personal use. No part may be edited, amended, extracted or reproduced in any form whatsoever. It may not be distributed or made available to others without prior permission in writing from the publisher.

The publisher and author have made every effort to contact copyright holders. If anyone believes that their copyright material has not been correctly acknowledged, please contact the publisher, who will be pleased to rectify the omission.

The moral right of the author has been asserted in accordance with the Copyrights, Designs and Patents Act 1988.

ISBN 978 1 78482 125 8 (print edition)
ISBN 978 1 78482 126 5 (digital edition)

British Library Cataloguing in Publication Data
A catalogue record for this book is available from the British Library

Original text and cover design by Toucan Graphic Design Ltd revised by Kate Griffith
Typeset by Marlinzo Services, Frome
Printed and bound in Great Britain by CPI Group, Croydon

Contents

Introduction ... 1
Divide and conquer ... 5
Move the snail ... 9
Feel the force ... 12
Iceberg ahoy! ... 16
Group hug ... 18
Divine compost ... 23
If wishes were changes ... 27
No one ever thinks they are rich ... 30
Plant a tree under whose shade you do not expect to sit ... 33
Begin with the basics ... 37
Thanks a million ... 39
The changing nature of stability ... 43
The porcupine principle ... 46
Hidden treasure ... 50
How much did your house cost? ... 55
'From this distance they couldn't hit an ele...' ... 59
The map is not the territory ... 63
Jackanory, tell me a story ... 66
Charisma, passion, leadership and illusion ... 70
Assessing the risks of risk assessments ... 74
Even a blind chicken finds some grain ... 78
The latent functions of work ... 82
OK, let's do the maths, shall we? ... 87
And this too shall pass away ... 90
My bubble, you squeak ... 93
Realpolitik ... 97
Emotional intelligence ... 102
Planning your way out of a bag ... 106
To change is to honour the tradition ... 110

Poor people can't afford cheap goods	114
Svengali fundraising	118
Overcoming your fundraising phobia	122
Think product not process	127
The altruism–exchange axis	130
Numbers ask questions, they don't give answers	134
Giving is good for you	138
'I don't care about the money; I just want to be wonderful'	142
Creativity in mysterious places	146
Sanctified by use: can money be laundered?	149
The five essential truths	154
Never cease exploring	158
References and notes	161

'And philanthropy seems to me to have become simply the refuge of people who wish to annoy their fellow-creatures'

Oscar Wilde

About the Directory of Social Change

At the Directory of Social Change (DSC), we believe that the world is made better by people coming together to serve their communities and each other. For us, an independent voluntary sector is at the heart of that social change and we exist to support charities, voluntary organisations and community groups in the work they do. Our role is to:

- **provide practical information** on a range of topics from fundraising to project management in both our printed publications and our e-books;
- **offer training** through public courses, events and in-house services;
- **research funders** and maintain a subscription database, *Funds Online*, with details on funding from grant-making charities, companies and government sources;
- **offer bespoke research** to voluntary sector organisations in order to evaluate projects, identify new opportunities and help make sense of existing data;
- **stimulate debate and campaign** on key issues that affect the voluntary sector, particularly to champion the concerns of smaller charities.

We are a registered charity ourselves but we self-fund most of our work. We charge for services but cross-subsidise those which charities particularly need and cannot easily afford.

Visit our website **www.dsc.org.uk** to see how we can help you to help others and have a look at **www.fundsonline.org.uk** to see how DSC could improve your fundraising. Alternatively, call our friendly team at **020 4526 5995** to chat about your needs or drop us a line at **cs@dsc.org.uk**.

Foreword

I first met Jonathan when I ran supporter appeals in the fundraising team at Oxfam over 30 years ago. As an undergraduate, he came to do work experience.

Oxfam was like a fundraising university in those days. It was pioneering so much cutting-edge stuff that it delivered wisdom without even realising it. Even so, I remember Jonathan sorting out my mailing spreadsheets, among other things, with a speed and brilliance that made my jaw drop.

We taught him everything we knew about supporters and fundraising appeals, and he soaked it up like a sponge. He has built on that foundation and learned so much more since then. Which is why this book is a pint-size gem packed with lessons from Jonathan's long years of working at the coalface of raising money.

He has distilled his fundraising knowledge in a breadth of leadership roles from hospices to education of deaf people, from youth centres to the Church of England. However, this book is not a boring fundraising textbook; it is packed with Jonathan's personal stories, his wit and his wisdom. It is the sheer humanity of the book that makes it stand out.

It reminds us – in an age of artificial intelligence, digital appeals and clever data analysis – that fundraising is about people. Indeed, one of the first things I was told when I went to work at Oxfam was that 'people give to people', and that the job of fundraising and fundraisers is to join the two.

The Porcupine Principle takes that simple but fundamental idea and builds on it with over 30 years of Jonathan's fundraising experience.

I hope you enjoy soaking up Jonathan's lifetime of fundraising insight.

Joe Saxton, Founder, Hey Hey Joe

Introduction

There is an inherent irony in the fact that I was once Chief Executive of a charity that ran a school. I spent most of my childhood doing my best to avoid school and was so good at avoiding it that I ended up with calamitous A-Levels as a result. Having surveyed my career choices at that time, I declined the kind offer to turn my temporary job in the fertiliser section of the local garden centre into a permanent one and headed 'down south' to Cambridgeshire College of Arts and Technology. I studied for an HND in Business and Finance (HND standing for, as I am sure you know, Have No Degree, as opposed to Higher National Diploma). While studying one of the modules on this course, I had the novel experience of discovering a subject that I really liked. I vividly remember the conversation with my dad, who, I should point out, was a chartered accountant at the time. Me: 'Dad, I have finally found a subject I actually like! I actually want to go to the lessons! I really and honestly enjoy it!' Dad: 'That's great, what is it?' Me: 'Marketing!' Cue muffled sounds of phone being dropped, various expletives, then long pause. Dad: 'Was there absolutely nothing else that interested you?'

I stumbled into fundraising when I had to take a six-month marketing work placement as part of my HND. I wrote to the chair of Oxfam asking for a job, and enclosed some suggested adverts they might like to use. These involved cutting pictures out of a magazine and then using

Letraset to create the copy (for younger readers, Letraset was a distant precursor to desktop publishing, but not nearly as good and much slower to create because you manually rubbed each letter on to the paper). Sadly, they did not use the adverts, but they did use me, and that started my fundraising life.

Many people are very sniffy about fundraising, but I think it is a great and important thing to do because it is an essential part of enabling charities to carry out the vital work they do. Of course, those who deliver the work of the charity are critical, but you cannot make social change without people and things, and they both cost money. Fundraising, by paid or voluntary fundraisers, is the fuel for your charity's philanthropic engine.

Many people are very disdainful about marketing too, which is probably more understandable. I know I shouldn't, because it's easy to see it as a bit shallow and trivial, but I have always loved marketing, and I can't help it. When I was a child, I loved the free figurines you used to get in cereal packets: the sense of excitement as you opened the packet to discover whether you had the one you really, really wanted. Even then, I think, I knew I was being had, but I was happy to be 'had' if it was this much fun.

So many of the conundrums and difficulties to do with fundraising are to do with the fact that it uses very similar techniques and principles to those found in consumer marketing, but it is communicating far more significant and profound issues. It is not about washing powder, fashion or music; it is about the eradication of suffering, injustice or hunger. Can things that are so divergent really use the same means of research, development, delivery, communication, monitoring and evaluation?

For better or worse, I think they can.

Since I left college, I have used my marketing skills to fundraise for many different charities. I have worked for massive multinational charities and tiny local ones. I have worked in generic 'any kind of fundraising' roles and also in specialised ones. I have worked at the coalface, actually asking people for money, as well as managing others who did the asking. I have been paid to do it or frequently given my time for free. The 41 chapters that follow are a distillation of my experiences in fundraising, which I hope will encourage you in your fundraising, whomever it is for and in whatever way you do it, and inspire you to achieve more than you ever thought you could.

If you are reading this introduction in the hope that it will explain what the porcupine principle is, then, first, congratulations on reading this far. Second, I am not going to tell you, you will have to read the relevant chapter (after you have bought the book, obviously). But I will tell you that it is a simple concept that looks at how you can communicate your charity's work in a powerful and memorable way but that does not steamroller the emotions of the potential supporter. This is one of the great fundraising challenges: how do you communicate the importance of what you do without either boring the supporter or traumatising them? The porcupine principle, like the rest of the book that bears its name, is there to help you to be a tippety-toppety fundraiser.

What charitable organisations do is very often fantastic; and because fundraising is needed to help them do what they do, that makes fundraising fantastic too. It is a terrific thing to be a part of, whether you are involved with a charity like Oxfam or your school's fundraising committee. We are all involved in the same business: leaving the world in a better state than we found it. Fundraising enables the world to be a little bit fairer, more just, more peaceful, kinder, more compassionate, healthier and more understanding. If you are reading this book, then you are probably already part of this work. I hope this book helps you to do it even better.

Divide and conquer

When is £1,000 not £1,000? Easy. When it is four times £250. One of the problems of raising money is that the amount needed can just seem too terrifying. A large part of fundraising lies in motivating and encouraging people to believe that the target is attainable. I was once asked by a 16-year-old how she could raise £1,000 to help fund her summer holiday working with street children in Ethiopia. She was, and I am sure still is, a genuinely inspiring person to be around. Her fear for the project was not for her own safety, or the trauma of what she might see and experience, but for how she was going to raise the money.

One thousand pounds just seemed too daunting a figure, particularly if you were starting from nothing and had a weekly disposable income of about £10. However, it is important that you are not intimidated into inactivity by an ambitious total, whether it is £1,000 or £1 million. How did she raise £1,000? She divided the grand into four equal amounts of £250. Already that made it look better. Then she looked at her different 'giving circles'.

Giving circles are like a Venn diagram (the only bit of maths I liked at school). They are different social groups to which you have access. One may be, say, a running club or a cricket team. Another may be your work colleagues. Another may be family and friends. Others may be religious groups, your neighbours or street, or locals at your favourite pub. Keep going like this, trying to define all your different giving circles (if, after half an hour, you have only written down 'my dog', then this exercise may not work for you). These giving circles will normally overlap to a certain extent (someone at your running club might also be a work colleague, for example). Sometimes, there will be several overlaps. The person at your running club who is also a work colleague might be a member of your local pub's darts team, a Rotarian and a near neighbour. Needless to say, such people are terribly important to you and should be fundraising friends for life if they are not already.

Next, you identify the giving circles that have some strong overlaps with others and where you know a large number of people. An important subtlety: your employer may employ 4,000 people, but you need to write down only the number who would know your name or at least recognise you. Pick the top four giving circles and set a target for each one. Then identify someone who can co-ordinate your fundraising for you within that giving circle. Get them on board, draw up a group of supporters within each giving circle, meet to plan how you will raise the money and then get on with it. Easy, you see.

A couple of explanatory points: first, if others see you as a good person, then people will give money to your cause, because really, in their eyes, they are giving money to you. Fundraising is thus an incentive to be seen as a good person. If you are known as 'that git from accounts', fundraising will not be easy. It is also why you need to look not at how many people are in your giving circle but at how many within that circle you know – or, more importantly, who know you.

Second, there are many reasons why a pub is a good place to plot and scheme your fundraising.

- It is an inherently social place, so your brain will be in a 'social setting' and so more attuned to what people will like.

- For some people, a social drink (alcoholic or otherwise) can help them think creatively and honestly.
- It is also a relaxed environment, where people can say what they think is a silly idea, but from which can come an idea of fundraising genius. People will sometimes say things in pubs that they will not say elsewhere.
- Pubs are also where people abide by that essential unwritten law: 'thou must be amusing at all times.' Fundraising without fun is still possible but not half as easy. For some, a pub can make the fundraising planning inherently more enjoyable (and also, of course, dramatically increases the chances of the pub becoming one of your four giving circles). But where you meet does not matter anywhere near as much as making sure the meeting itself is an enjoyable experience, so people will want to come back.

It is important, as well, to try to tailor your fundraising to your particular giving circle. The best fundraising ideas are developed within, not from without. What would work particularly well for that particular group? If you can think of something like this for your giving circle, then people will be more committed to the idea. If you follow this whole process above, you will go a long way towards reaching your target.

It would be remiss of me at this point not to mention a fundraising idea that worked wonderfully in a giving circle of a school parent–teachers association. I would dearly love this to have been my own idea, but alas it was not. One of the fundraising curses is to be struck down by organising a fundraising event. Notoriously time-consuming and frustrating, despite the marvellous social capital it creates, it can be as unpopular to attend as it is to organise. For many of us, time is more precious than money, and yet our fundraising still deals in the ever more expensive currency of time. Three hours to attend a school PTA barbecue is a significant sacrifice if you have no time to call your own.

Therefore, do everyone a favour and do not organise one at all. Instead, write to those you would have invited to your event (whatever it might be) and say – nicely – that you were going to organise an event and invite them to it, but, as you do not want to organise it and you know they do not want to come, let's create a win-win situation here by their giving you the money they would have spent at the event. Their social diary becomes a little less clogged, you suddenly find yourself with several hundred hours with which to do something useful that would otherwise have been spent on the event, and your charity has £1,000 in the bank. You will get away with this cheeky approach once, but it is probably the most efficient form of fundraising there is. If you make sure you ask them to complete a Gift Aid declaration at the same time, you are laughing all the way to the bank.

Move the snail

I think there is an irreconcilable cultural divide between those who love camping and those who do not. Occasionally, very occasionally, I could see the attraction. Waking to a beautiful sunny morning in outstandingly pretty countryside, the smell of bacon frying on the stove and the sound of the whistling kettle. This never happened of course, but that was the dream. Normally, the camping experience was not being able to sleep due to back ache caused by the slowly deflating air beds, then peering out of the tent to see, at best, a light drizzle that had soaked all the things you left out because you were sure it wasn't going to rain. It always amazed me that we, along with so many other people, worked hard to earn enough to have a decent standard of living, then happily gave up that standard of living to live in a muddy field without basic sanitation for a fortnight. And we called that a holiday.

Nonetheless, it seemed to be an essential rite of passage if you had small children – it's number 3 on the National Trust's '50 things to do before you are $11\frac{3}{4}$', for heaven's sake – and so camping holidays were had. This involved taking a staggering quantum of 'stuff', but happily one of my undeniable skills is packing, and so it was a test I relished in some ways. Arriving back from a three-week camping holiday in France, I once faced the daunting prospect of unloading a very well packed car and a ridiculously oversized roof box. At least twenty trips back and forth up the drive beckoned.

On my first trip, I noticed a snail right in the middle of the drive. I pondered the odds of me standing on the snail as I traipsed back and forth and concluded its life expectancy was not good. Each time I brought in another load, I tried to avoid the snail, which I could not see, because I was carrying stuff in. After about the eighth trip I found myself, ludicrously, resenting the snail. Why did it have to be there, of all places? Why couldn't it be just a yard to the left or right? But oh no, it had to be in the very most awkward place imaginable. Wasn't it hard enough bringing in three weeks' worth of holiday clobber without having to tiptoe around a snail?

I pondered whether I should deliberately take out the snail – a pre-emptive strike – so I didn't add to the stress of the task by dancing around it. But then, I would feel bad about killing a snail just for my convenience. I started to resent this hideous Hobson's choice, knowing quite well that I would have to carry the added stress of the snail avoidance strategy rather than living with the guilt of the snail murder for my own convenience. I should clarify, I was very tired at the time.

Eventually, I finished unpacking, with this dilemma unresolved. Sat on the sofa with a restorative cup of tea, and still grumbling about the insensitive snail and why it was tormenting me (did I mention I was very tired?), I thought of a third option – just move the snail. I wish this idea had come to me after the first trip, but sadly I did not, as is so often the case. On the rare occasions when I have a blinding flash of insight, I normally have it just too late. Plus ça change, as the French probably don't say.

Trying to find the solution to a problem does often require lateral thinking, whatever that means, but, critically, it requires time. So often we rush our thinking and that rushing is where we lose the opportunities for insight. Sometimes this stampede towards a solution is unavoidable – external forces demand it – but, looking back, it is surprising how often it has been self-imposed. Perhaps due to an eagerness to solve a problem and move on, or a fear of the complexity of the problem, we fast forward the decision-making and it rarely ends well when we do so.

I decided to move the snail anyway; I figured I could give it a helping hand after feeling such mean thoughts about it. I hauled myself up from the sofa, went outside to the drive and picked up the shell. It was empty.

Feel the force

What motivates your donors to give to your cause? It is so important that you try to get inside their heads. It can often be a pretty harrowing experience. It is easy to assume why people give, and those assumptions are normally something to do with how marvellous a fundraiser you are. The reality is that people sometimes give in a very confused way. Here we are thinking they are like some form of social army, ready to win the battles of injustice, when sometimes they give for, frankly, quite muddled reasons. They may not be really sure why they give or whether it makes a difference. In my experience, some people give despite being convinced that it does not make any difference at all. It just makes them feel better to say they have tried and failed to make a difference, rather than not to have tried at all. I remember when I worked for a Christian charity, I sent a questionnaire to our supporters asking why they gave. Among the expected replies was a gem: 'I used to have a faith, but now don't, but admire those who do, so I keep giving.' That was hardly somebody supporting us because they lived and breathed our values, was it? So do not have too high an expectation for the motivations of donors. Remember, charitable giving for most people is a tiny part of their lives, coming way down on the list of things they think about. We are the sad, tragic types who agonise over these things.

Broadly, you can say that there are four main motivations for giving, which all, by happy coincidence, begin with the same letter.

Grace

The way it used to be. There is a donation box in a special needs school with a plaque on it that reads 'Given by a governor in the hope of acts of kind benevolence'. Marvellous. People were motivated to give because they had done well out of life and believed it was a way of expressing their gratitude for their financial state. There are still people who give because of this motivation, but they are dwindling in number. You could argue that Bill Gates is motivated by grace to give. There are remarkable similarities between the present mega-rich philanthropists and the Victorian ones, who founded so many of our schools, hospitals and libraries. Grace givers believe they are under no compulsion to give, but they just want to. This message is the opposite of the hectoring guilt message that makes you feel compelled to give (see next motivation). It could be caricatured as 'it would be awfully sweet if you could be so generous as to help out'.

Guilt

Sir Bob Geldof has clearly been a stupendously good fundraiser, particularly during Live Aid. I would say he has a genius-level ability at using the power of guilt as a motivator for fundraising. It is a simple and blunt message that could be caricatured as. 'They are poor because you are rich. If you have any shred of humanity, you will realise that it is tantamount to murder to spend your cash on clothes/eating out/TV/holiday (delete as applicable) when you could give it to save a life from a certain, painful and pointless death.' The merit of this motivation is that it is, at its heart, right.

The downside is that it increasingly alienates people who object to being lectured. It can also lead to a donor who does give £20 feeling it is insignificant because they have not sold their house and given the proceeds to the poor. It can also lead to fundraisers becoming and appearing unbearably smug. Guilt motivation messages from fundraisers can be seen as 'why aren't you more like me?' It is somewhat of its time too, a hangover from the 1980s, when it was the dominant fundraising discourse; people's attitude to charity has moved on to...

Growth

This is *so* now. Charitable giving is actually just a way of expressing your inner values and of becoming the person you aspire to be. You know you are a kind, generous, compassionate person, but, alas, in life you are heavily in demand, your time is not your own and you realise that your skills are limited. However much you may want to, you may never be a nurse, a youth worker, an advice worker and so on. Nonetheless, your donation can enable someone else to do this, so that is what you do. By giving, you are growing as a human being because you are achieving the change you want to see in the world. There is loads of mileage in this. This growth motivation is clever because it can be assimilated effortlessly into a lifestyle that stays much the same. There are no nagging doubts that you should be doing more and no divorcing of your giving from the rest of your life; it is just an extension of your circle of influence and fits perfectly within your normal way of living.

Gratitude

This is a hugely powerful motivation. One of the beauties of fundraising is the way that it brings together such disparate sectors. For example, both cancer charities and educational institutions use this motivation, often in very simple, if not blunt, ways. Any discerning reader can often understand the coded messages: 'You don't want others to suffer like your gran did, do you?' or 'You've made yourself stinking rich largely because of the qualification we gave you, so pay up.' Gratitude can be a fantastic motivation for giving because it is so simple and uncomplicated. 'Thanks for caring for my mum. I just wanted to say thanks.' – it is the nearest fundraising equivalent to being given a bunch of flowers. Where fundraisers need to tread carefully is when there is a danger that the donor associates their depth of thanks, or loss, with the amount they give. Often donors may torture themselves over the inadequacy of their gift. It is incredibly important to acknowledge the act of giving more than the size of the gift. I believe that is always true, but it is even more so with this motivation.

So what motivates you to give, and what motivates those who give to your cause? See if you can analyse the way you raise money and the way you describe your cause. What motivation are you trying to encourage and is that consistent with the aims and values of your charity? Do you need to try something different in order to reach different people? There is plenty to ponder on. And if you can think of other motivations, then do let me know.

Iceberg ahoy!

Looking back on a long and undistinguished fundraising career, I must have given fundraising advice to around 50 charities, I would think. They would often approach me in some financial distress. I would ask them what the problem was, and the answer would normally be 'money, or lack of it'. So, did I give them some inspired advice and guidance on fundraising which brought in the money that they needed? Without exception, I did not. This was because, also without exception, the problem was not a fundraising one.

Imagine an organisation's ailments are an iceberg. Fundraising is the bit you see above the waterline. The other ailments, which dwarf the fundraising ones, are hidden from view but are far more dangerous. The truth is that, in many cases, if charities are well run, then money will find its way to them. It often takes a good fundraiser to bring it in, but the money can still be found. If a charity cannot find the money no matter how hard it tries, there is probably something fundamentally wrong.

Here are a few non-fundraising reasons why charities may not have enough money:

- They spend too much of what they've got. Costs have not been controlled and investments have not been made in more efficient systems and processes than those they have used in the past. Such charities

do not need to receive more money, they need to spend less. In my experience, this is the most common cause of a 'fundraising' crisis.
- There is no longer any demand for what they do. What the charity delivers is no longer what people need, so no amount of communication will elicit support.
- They have not taken people with them. They have become isolationist and not explained to supporters what they are doing and why. People no longer understand what the charity does, and so they do not give money to it. Often previous donors may have been treated with such contempt that they have given up and supported someone else.
- Someone else does what they do better, so people give to them instead.
- They have turned the charity into a club for trustees, volunteers and staff rather than placing the needs of their beneficiaries at the heart of what they do.
- They have treated their staff and/or volunteers so abysmally that turnover is huge and, eventually, that means that there are so many unhappy former staff and/or volunteers within the community that the community itself turns against the charity.

Fundraising cannot be isolated from the other crucial facets of what makes a successful charity. That is why, when you face a financial crisis, the astute decision would be to review the whole operation, not just the fundraising activities. Smartening up the tip of the iceberg does not make the rest of the iceberg disappear.

Group hug

To be a great fundraiser you really do need to have an extraordinary array of skills and abilities. You need to be highly creative, yet extremely organised. You need to be able to speak to hundreds, yet also be stimulating company with one or two. You need to be spontaneous and flexible but also a good planner. Fundraising is a series of contradictory and paradoxical skill sets, which, it could be argued, are only attainable by one person if that person has a tenuous hold on reality.

Let me reassure you: you do not have to be *all* of the above (and more) to be a really good fundraiser. In some ways, it actually helps if you are not. I find big social gatherings traumatic, yet I enjoy speaking at them because I am a curious combination of being both shy and a show-off. I cannot do the most basic mental arithmetic, I am not at all organised, and I have a complete inability to remember names or indeed navigate to anywhere. I argued successfully with my boss that by depriving me of satellite navigation my employer was discriminating against me because of this inability that I could do nothing about. Clearly, I must be persuasive, but often I might ruin it all by changing my mind mid-argument and then amuse myself by seeing if anyone notices. Despite my inability to remember names and navigate, I managed to hold down a regional fundraising job for 18 months. Perhaps this fact does not reflect well on either me or the charity concerned, but it shows that you do not need the full skill set to find a meaningful role within fundraising.

That is the central point. Fundraising is not an individual discipline; it is a team activity. This is why so many 'lone fundraisers' in small charities give up; they are being asked to do too many contradictory things and they do not have anyone with whom to share the roles.

I was once asked to give a talk on '10 top tips on fundraising'. Instead, I gave a talk on 'fantasy fundraising', which showed how my 11 favourite footballers all had essential fundraising attributes (showing again my inability in mental arithmetic and indeed an inability to follow simple instructions). It led to many a healthy debate (could footballers George Best and Eric Cantona really have played well together?), but more importantly, it got the point across that good fundraising needs both a safe pair of hands like goalkeeper Ray Clemence and lovely hair like French footballer/model David Ginola (or something like that).

So, what are the essential roles that any fundraising team needs? I think you could say the following caricatures are exaggerated forms of the different kinds of skill sets you need, and you may well be able to think of more.

Precious artiste

They spend most of their time off in 'la la land'. In meetings, they draw numerous diagrams with circles and arrows pointing everywhere that no one else can understand. Often they do not have a practical bone in their body, can be quite emotional, occasionally dogmatic and become misty-eyed when they talk about an idea they have had. They will normally blurt this idea out at inopportune moments, have a total inability to follow an agenda and frequently say the word 'amazing'. I am one of these. Honestly, I am. It is amazing. 'Precious artistes' are rare and temperamental, but they are essential. While they rarely come up with the finished product, they are pivotal in the early stages when truly great fundraising ideas emerge.

Nerd

A nerd is cruelly mocked by the precious artiste, who is secretly frightened of the nerd's apparent grip on themselves and reality. Nerds think risk assessments are 'perfectly sensible' and talk about something being a 'wise precaution'. Their favourite mantra is 'to fail to plan is to plan to fail'. They are absolutely essential to taking the precious artiste's ideas and making them work. However, they need to be watched, because if they critique an idea too early in its development, they can kill off the creative energy that is essential in developing the idea into something that might work. If they do this, the precious artiste will then burst into tears and stomp off.

Show-off

Most people are absolutely mortified at the idea of standing up in front of anyone to talk about anything. However, a small minority positively thrive on it, and often they are the same ones who are quite shy and not good social mixers, which can make them hard to spot. Show-offs are very good at doing the uncomfortable parts of fundraising – like asking for money. They are real adrenaline junkies, who love the nervous energy that comes from 'performing'. The marvellous actor Bill Nighy portrayed this kind of character exactly when he said, 'To have 400 people laugh at the same time, you'd go to your grave trying to get it right'. Good show-offs are amazing (that word again). They can somehow wriggle their way into people's souls and hearts to form an emotional connection between the charity and the supporter.

Bean-counter

Fundraising is about raising as much money as possible for as little cost as possible. Every fundraising team needs someone to point this out regularly. Fundraising ideas can develop a life of their own, soaring away from financial reality like an untethered kite on the beach. The bean-counters keep people on track. They are very important, because it is raising money that really motivates fundraisers more than having a good time. The bean-counter ensures that motivation is as high as it can be.

Schmoozer

What is your worst nightmare? I know mine. It is being at a business networking lunch. Even the thought of it brings me out in a cold sweat. Being both shy and unable to remember people's names is not a good combination for a networker. Some, however, positively thrive on meeting new people. They skip along to networking lunches and social groups like spring lambs, bouncing up to total strangers and having an absolute ball. Every fundraising team needs a schmoozer who can get crucial people to support you, whether in business, social groups, politics, religious groups, sporting groups or other social circles.

Gopher

It is approaching midnight, and it is dark and cold. A euphoric group of fundraisers walks off into the distance celebrating their fire-walking success. They leave behind a small group of people with black bin liners who have to clear up the drinks, hot dogs, candy floss, sweets and all the other rubbish that comes with fundraising events. Ten minutes in, it starts to rain. Hard. Twenty minutes later, the gophers are soaked to the skin, but the site is spotless. It is not the euphoric fundraisers who will persuade the owners of the venue to hold another fundraising event there free of charge. It is the gophers. Fundraising teams often treat gophers terribly. If they acknowledge them at all, they can be deeply patronising – 'oh aren't you doing a smashing job!' – but gophers are an equal and essential part of a successful fundraising team and should be adored for what they are.

Lion-tamer

Last, you need some poor soul who has to bring together all the above into a coherent team. They need to have terrific interpersonal skills, courage and stamina. They need to keep people on track and ensure that everyone is doing what they said they would do. At the end of a fundraising event or campaign, they need to bring the team together and thank them for their individual contributions. They need to keep focusing the team members on the cause they are raising funds for, so that they maintain a sense of perspective and direction.

No one person can do all of these things, and it would be absurd to think they could. Fundraising is so multi-faceted that it absolutely demands teams rather than individuals. The real trick as a fundraiser is to know what you can do and what you cannot, and to be comfortable with that. You then need to be good at spotting your lion-tamers, gophers, bean-counters and the rest. Finally, most importantly, you need to charm them into getting involved. You see, it is all quite straightforward and simple. Amazing!

Divine compost

Being a part-time and very amateur theologian tends to mean seeing things in a slightly different and often quirky way. There is a theology of divine compost that, once understood, could revolutionise the way you ask for money (especially when you are asking for legacies). Think for a moment about how you try and persuade people to give your organisation money. How much time do you spend trying to understand your cause, and how much time do you spend trying to understand your donor? Why would anyone want to hand over their hard-earned cash to you? If you think it is because of your stunning powers of communication, I am afraid I must bring you some bad news. It isn't. It is probably much more likely that they give to your charity because of some connection in their own life, either current or past, or because your charity embodies some of the values with which they agree.

I know this is a fairly big question (and, I imagine, you may need time to think about it), but what exactly do you think your life is for? Why do you exist (if you believe that you do)? Or do you think there is no reason? Is it just chance? Even if you can't answer that, what should we be doing now that we are here? How do we measure success (if we think success is important, of course)? Does it depend on how much money we have? How many friends, how many children, lovers or pets? I would argue that there is a fairly dominant way of thinking in our society that can be broadly summed up as selfish. Life is about getting what you can, about desiring and acquiring, and about experiencing more than your peers. Divine compost is a marvellous antidote to that, because, by focusing on our mortality, we are given a different perspective on our present lives.

Memento mori used to do the same thing. In the 18th century, people would have a pleasing still-life painting hanging on the wall – of flowers, books, a musical instrument, perhaps, or a basket of fruit. And there, in the middle of this charming scene, would be a human skull. The purpose of such a painting was to remind people that time is fleeting (images of clocks used to denote the same), that our worldly possessions will rot and decay, as indeed will we. Therefore, because our mortality is an unarguable truth, we should use this perspective to guide our lives now. Frankly, who cares what we own? It all counts for nought. So, what does not rot or decay? Well, in a strange way, we don't. Stay with me here; I am not trying to convert you to anything, except perhaps to make you look at the world from a slightly different angle. It can probably be best explained by a quick dip into my own life history.

I adored my Granddad and was incredibly sad when he died at the fabulous age of 92. Staying with my grandparents was a highlight of my childhood. I loved everything about it: playing dominoes, watching Dewsbury rugby league club lose or practising my golf putting on the back lawn. I do not play dominoes, watch Dewsbury lose at rugby or play golf any more. However, I do try to be like my granddad. He used to let me win at dominoes in a very clever way, so that I really thought I had beaten him fair and square. I learned to do the same thing when playing table football with my daughters. I learnt from him to be self-deprecating, to be stoical and brave (better on the former than the latter), to avoid being overly dramatic, to accept who I am and to be comfortable in my skin. I hope some of these traits have been passed on to my own children. These traits did not just appear as if by magic; they were inherited. My Granddad is divine compost because he has grown these good things in his children and grandchildren. It is because we teach these things to our children that they will in turn teach them to theirs; the impact is eternal.

What has this to do with fundraising? Everything. What we do does not just affect us, it affects everyone. When we are selfish, we show our children how to be selfish, and they will in turn show their children. When we are generous and kind, we affect generation after generation. What we do matters. Giving money is not some pointless exercise to assuage comfortable, middle-class guilt. It makes a difference and will continue to make a difference in perpetuity.

How do you incorporate this within your fundraising message? By making sure that you show how generosity ripples outwards. Do not stop at saying a donation will take a homeless person off the streets. Talk about what they will do when they are off the streets. Who will they meet and what will they do? What acts of goodness will they now be able to do? Much charity work is made up of mechanisms, and mechanisms are pretty dull to explain. But what happens because of those mechanisms? That is when the message gets interesting.

I used to be a fundraiser for a hospice, and I know there is not much easier fundraising than fundraising for a hospice, but it still had its moments. One of the frustrations was how reluctant we were to talk about our patients as people, rather than disease carriers. For me, one of the big things about improving a patient's quality of life was the ripple effect it had on their family and friends. Just think of those conversations that could take place only because the pain had been controlled. Think about the birthdays, weddings and christenings that they would not have been able to attend if the hospice had not been good at what it did. It gave the patients a chance to enjoy so many things, and it also gave their families and friends a greater opportunity to enjoy spending time with them.

I do not know why, I have never really understood it, but charities are often incredibly reluctant to acknowledge the human dimension in their work. It really does not matter what the charity does, it will still affect people. Someone said to me recently that all of my fundraising was for people, but how on earth would I raise money for art? This sums up our fundraising problems perfectly. Art is about people too, it's made by people, for people. Everything is about people, and charities and charitable giving are about people as well. Understanding divine compost will enable you to remember that.

> *I lay in dust life's glory dead,*
> *And from the ground there blossoms red*
> *Life that shall endless be.*
>
> George Matheson

If wishes were changes

The late and much mourned Nanci Griffith wrote and sang many beautiful songs. A personal favourite was the song 'If wishes were changes'. In the song, she laments that, much as we may wish things to change, it doesn't mean they will. If wishes were changes, then life would be wonderful; if we could wish away the things that are wrong in the world, then it would be a much happier place to be. But the reality of course is that this isn't possible. Our wishes do not always lead to changes; in fact, they often do not. It is easy, if we want something badly enough, to think our wish has become a change. Particularly, I would argue, if we work in a values-driven world, where that desire to change and improve lives is an enormous motivator. It is easy for that desire to slip from driving change into believing change has happened when it has not. The more immediate the need, the higher the stakes, the more likely this is to happen.

Charlotte Higgins, in her book *Under Another Sky: Journeys in Roman Britain*, tells a compelling story of how easy it is to believe something has happened when, in fact, it hasn't. In 1904, Edward Nicholson, the head of Oxford's Bodleian Library, was attempting to decipher fragmentary letters scratched on a lead tablet that had been found among Roman remains in Bath. He published the translation, and it was an astonishing discovery. This was a letter between two Christians, way before the Christian faith was thought to have been established in England. In it, the writer

Vinisius urged the recipient Nigra to be 'strong in Jesus' and warned her against heresies.

Ninety years after Nicholson's translation, Dr Roger Tomlin reviewed the photographs of the find to make his own discovery – Nicholson had read the tablet upside down. It was actually a curse tablet, written to implore the gods to curse someone who had stolen something from them by denying them sleep until the stolen object was returned.

The juxtaposition between what Nicholson thought, or hoped, it was and what it actually was is hilarious. It is difficult to think how he could have got it more wrong. Nicholson had not deliberately set out to deceive. Rather, he found what he wanted to see. How often do we do the same?

Tomlin says the story of the curse tablet and Nicholson is a handy reminder to him to always check he is reading things the right way up. It is not a bad advice for us too. Sometimes I have so wanted a fundraising initiative to be a success that I have effectively been looking at the data upside down. We sometimes remain adamant that a pet fundraising initiative we have piloted is still genius even if the data says it was a turkey. The data must be wrong, because we are so madly in love with this stroke of fundraising genius, we can't comprehend it might not actually work. So then we convince ourselves that the problem is not the idea or the initiative or the project, but the way we are delivering it. We're not trying hard enough, we're not prioritising it enough, we're not resourcing it enough. The unfortunate reality is that the force of inertia or antipathy for an idea from others can be as strong as whatever energy we can muster to promote it. So, we end up proving Newton's third law of motion, which, in case it has temporarily slipped your mind, says that 'for every action, there is an equal and opposite reaction'. Putting in more energy and more resource to a flawed project just grows the resistance to it. We need to step back, be objective and check our zeal for this fundraising idea isn't obscuring our vision to the extent that we are misreading what the data is telling us.

As fundraisers we can be particularly susceptible to thinking wishes are changes, because we are desperate to see change and we acutely feel the pressure to deliver that change. When my current team recently did a strengths profile exercise, one of the most frequent strengths the team members had was being a legacy builder – we want to make the world a better place, to leave it better than we found it. In my view, it is understandable that this driver might then lead us to see a changed world when it is not, or not as much as we would like.

In the 'Group hug' chapter (see page 18), I talk about when there is a time to listen to those who can take a step back and critique things, and look at things dispassionately, and this is one of those moments. When the idea is in motion, but the data shows it's not exactly working, this is when data needs to be centre stage. It is perfectly possible to be so transfixed with an idea that we ignore the data that tells us no one else is. We need to see the reality, and stepping back to objectively look at the data helps us not confuse our wishes for changes.

No one ever thinks they are rich

I'll let you in on one of my favourite fundraising secrets; you can really have fun with this one, I promise. It is a very simple exercise that is incredibly important for understanding how people think about money. Get your fundraising team or group together and ask them this question:

Which would you prefer?

a) To earn £50,000 per year when the average salary is £25,000 per year

or

b) To earn £100,000 per year when the average salary is £200,000 per year

I am chortling to myself as I write this, thinking about the fun I have had with people's responses. It really depends on how honest the members of your group are, but when people are asked this question, the overwhelming majority answer a). People would happily forgo a doubling of their salary in preference for getting double what other people get.

This exercise illustrates the fact that people's attitude to money is relative, not absolute. Our satisfaction with what we have is totally determined by what we have in relation to what others have. My car was fine until the neighbours got a new car and now I think my car is junk. My old TV, that weighed as much as a hippo with a gland problem, was fine until my father-in-law bought his flat screen television. It is the 'politics of envy' that spurs people on to earn more, even if we do not like thinking of it in this way. Therefore, when people earn more, they just discover more ways of spending, and only the super-rich run out of different ways of spending money.

Back in my youthful fundraising days, when I earned the princely sum of £36 a week, I used to marvel at the salaries I read about in the papers. I never pretended that £36 a week was enough to live on but thought that, if I had double that, I would be very comfortably off, taking me to the dizzy heights of about £5,000 a year. This meant that, if someone was on £100,000 a year, they would then have about £95,000 to give away every single year! Remarkable. So, all I needed to do was to find a rich person by looking under 'R' in the *Yellow Pages* and tell them to cough up.

Looking back on my naivety, it makes me smile. The world looks unbelievably different when you have mortgages, car loans, and children to feed and clothe. The reality is that, as our wealth increases, so do the opportunities and expectations for spending. What we define as 'reasonable' expenditure changes with our personal circumstance. 'Wealthy people', a relative term in itself, simply do not have money swilling around in their current accounts that they are clueless as to how to spend. They plan and account for the money in just the same way I did for my £36.

Therefore, when you are asking someone to give money, it does not matter how wealthy they are, they are still going to have to forgo some planned expenditure or planned saving. It is still money that they intended to keep or spend *on themselves*. Fundraising is telling people that they need to give that money that they intended to keep for themselves, or spend on themselves, to someone else. It is not about telling them that they have got 'loads of money' and you are happy to take some of that irritating cash off their hands – cash they can never find a use for anyway.

The consequence of all of this is that the fundraising message needs to be remarkably similar, irrespective of the wealth of the person you are speaking to. It needs to focus on why it is more important that the charity's beneficiary has 'their money' than that they do. The beneficiary has a need that they cannot meet, and also the supporter has a moral obligation or desire to try to meet that need. It is quite simple, really. If you try to see fundraising as some form of 'class war' where your job is to screw the rich, I am afraid you will not succeed. Fundraising is about getting inside the head of a donor, and understanding their attitude to money is a key part of that.

Plant a tree under whose shade you do not expect to sit

There are undoubtedly times when fundraising can be fun. It is an inherently edifying business, helping people out, and as so much of fundraising is sociable, and people like being sociable, it is almost difficult not to enjoy it sometimes. However, I do have a problem with people who tend to see fundraising as an end in itself, as if the very activity was so exciting and such fun that we should do it whether it raises money or not. Perhaps I worry too much, but fundraising to me is always haunted by the spectre of failure and the consequences of that failure. For that reason, I can never be all that excited by the process.

What I really can be excited about are the consequences of the fundraising. Fundraising is about changing lives. Money is an essential means for us to be a caring, compassionate and just society. We need the money to pay for salaries, photocopiers, boilers, furniture and all the other things we need to make a difference. The real excitement for me is that without fundraising there would not be a more caring, compassionate and just society. Fundraising is a simply marvellous activity in that the fruits of it are so incredibly wholesome and beneficial. To me, there is nothing that comes close to it, and I suppose that is why I have made a career out of it (if you can call my haphazard CV a career).

I do believe, though, that fundraising should not just be preoccupied with the here and now. If it is, it is easy for people to lose a very important sense of perspective. The danger of target setting is that the target can become the 'be all and end all' and nothing else matters. It does not matter how many are trampled in the crush to the finishing line, just that the finishing line is crossed. That might be OK in the short term, but if you ever need to go back to the ones you crushed, you will quickly regret the way you became too focused on your target. On my office notice board I used to have a sign that said 'The Lord loves a cheerful giver, but he'll settle for a begrudging one.' I am sure that is right, but the cost of coercing someone into being a reluctant giver is that they are much less likely to give again.

The real power of a charity, and thus your fundraising, lies in its ability to make long-term, irrevocable and deep change within our society. This is no makeover; this is about improving things for generations to come. The best way of looking at your fundraising is to look at it as a very long-term and profound project that requires patience and determination. When you are speaking to a supporter, you need to be thinking how your conversation will shape their giving for the next 20 years, not just for now. Put bluntly, are you carrying out your fundraising in a way that will make people want to give now, but then also give again and again? The 'here and now' is small beer, frankly; if you really want to change things, you need to get people on board for ever. As I said to one supporter, 'I don't want your money, I want your soul' and added a maniacal laugh to round it off. I was semi-serious, though – I really did want them to develop a life-long commitment to my cause.

This approach will require you to do your fundraising in a subtly different way. When you are planning, think beyond the initial target: consider what new opportunities it will open up in the future and write them down. Spend much more time 'not fundraising'. I spent hours of my working week 'not fundraising' with people who visited the charities where I worked. I never asked them for money and had no wish to do so. I wanted them to start the journey of understanding why my charity was important, and the contribution and the difference that they could make. I did not want them to think their contribution might only be to buy a raffle ticket; I wanted them to be in it for life.

The secret of this is to understand the difference between enthusiasm and motivation. People will give money to a charity either because they are enthused to do so or because they are motivated to do so. The enthusiasm can come from a charismatic fundraiser. A previous boss once remarked, with a mix of disdain and admiration (a difficult combination to get right), that a fundraising venture I had been involved in did not deserve to succeed at all but did so because people were blinded to its failings by my charisma. Sheer enthusiasm can get people on board. Most people want to be inspired, to be part of something significant, and a charismatic fundraiser can do this. But this is not sustainable, because the fundraiser's charisma will dry up, and the supporters will expect similar levels of excitement every time they give. Motivation is different. This is about the supporters themselves and how they get the energy to give from within themselves. This motivation comes through education, not only about the quality and importance of your charity but also about their essential role within it.

This requires real patience, and also an acknowledgement that, if I am to be honest, sometimes I must resist the urge to be seen as the essential fundraising linchpin who magics money out of nowhere. It can disempower supporters to the point that they think they are irrelevant to the fundraising work if you are not present. Fundraisers should be a window into a charity; they should be absolutely transparent so that most of the time you do not even notice they are there. They enable supporters to see in to a world that they know little or nothing about. They also enable the charity to see the outside world. So, they should not be a one-way mirror. Being a window is not exactly exciting or noteworthy, or something that gains public acclaim, but the charity, and therefore its beneficiaries, would be much gloomier without them. That should be enough in itself.

You will never get the credit for this 'eternal fundraising'. You will be well gone by the time the impact of your work becomes obvious. There will be no nice letters, awards, pay rises, fame and glory. In fact, to be truthful, people will probably never realise what you have done and the impact you have made. It will be a secret between you and your maker. However, being selfless does wonders for our self-worth (there's another paradox for you). Planting a tree to give you shade does not make you feel half as good as knowing that someone else will sit in the shade of a tree that you planted.

Begin with the basics

When my children were little, I had one of those treasured parental experiences you do not find in parenting manuals. My daughter was three years old and I asked her a question. She replied, 'uh?' I adopted a stern parental face, and she said, 'Oh, sorry, I mean, what?' I replied, 'I think the word you are looking for is "pardon".' 'Oh, whatever', she replied.

So, clearly, I am hardly one to preach about good manners, because I obviously struggled with instilling them into my own children. But if you are involved in fundraising, good manners really are absolutely essential. It is simply amazing how often fundraisers do not use them. Bad manners can be overt or subtle. The subtle bad manners manifest themselves in the way we can leave people with no moral option other than to do our bidding because of the emotional blackmail we lay on. The coded message we send is that we do not genuinely care about them and we just want their money. That is plain rude. These subtle ways may be harder to spot but can often be the most damaging.

That said, overt ways are very harmful too. What happened to good, old-fashioned 'please' and 'thank you'? So many charities do not acknowledge any donations, particularly small ones, and that leaves me baffled. How do you feel if you spend an age making tea and no one thanks you for it and then you are left to do the washing-up? Alternatively, how would you feel if someone did thank you for the tea but then said, 'Thanks for the tea, but we really need your help making tea tomorrow too.'? We would not treat people we know the way some charities have treated their donors, and how can that be right?

If some charities do acknowledge donations, then they often do so in the most remarkably begrudging way. As soon as the donation is acknowledged, they tell the donor off for not using Gift Aid, and when they have done that, the charities ask for more. What kind of message is that sending to their donors? Basically, I read that as saying 'We're acknowledging your donation, but it wasn't enough.' That, to me, is more bad manners.

One of the things you really should do is, just occasionally, ring up a donor to thank them for a donation rather than sending them a letter (assuming they have given you permission to do this, of course). They will be shocked to start off with, and a bit wary and suspicious of your motives, but when they realise it really is just a thank you, and not a call asking them to 'upgrade', they will be really pleased. They will be so pleased they will tell their friends about it too. It is a whole new niche: 'polite fundraising'; and I bet it has the best fundraising ratios going.

Thanks a million

Back in the dim and distant past, while working for St Luke's Hospice in Plymouth, I stumbled across an idea that I have been living off ever since. The hospice needed £1 million for a capital appeal. All great ideas normally come to people while having a bath, and, as I was pondering whether the damp patch in the ceiling was growing, I hit upon the idea of raising £1 million in 1 million seconds. I got quite excited about the whole idea, this race against time with people throwing money at the hospice as the seconds counted down. I even thought of the name: 'Thanks a million'.

Unfortunately for me, mental arithmetic has never been my strong suit. My guess was that 1 million seconds lasted somewhere around a couple of months. Before you chuckle at my inadequacy, you have a quick guess. Any idea? Not even close. A million seconds is about eleven and a half days. All of a sudden, the neat idea did not feel so neat after all. However, we were desperate, and I was naïve. I still had some deep psychological issues about needing to be needed, setting myself impossible targets to reaffirm my (false) perception of myself as a serial loser and so on. So, we went for it. Well, if raising £1,000 seems intimidating, then you have some idea of how scary raising £1 million is.

The appeal was knocked together in six weeks. In no way would I recommend this. It is a digression, but I reckon every pound raised took a minute off my life, which works out as about 23 years off my life (OK, it is actually only two years off my life, but that is still excessive in my book). What you are doing is simply too important to be attempted in such a reckless manner.

One of the aspects of the appeal was a TV advertising campaign. We were told in advance when the adverts would go out, so that we could ensure that there would be people there to answer our (ten) phones in our 'call centre' (the fundraising office). I had worked late that day ('worked late' in Devon means, ooh, until about 5.15pm) when suddenly every phone started ringing. The buggers had put our advert out at a different time. I do not know whether you have ever tried to answer ten phones simultaneously, but I can tell you, it is not easy. So, I hurtled down the corridor, shouting like a crazed idiot for volunteers for an essential job for which no training would be given and which would start now. Thanks to the cooks and cleaners, we answered most of the calls. I look back and laugh now, but the whole twelve days was like that. Total madness. So don't do it. Really, don't do it.

There were a couple of neat tricks with the appeal that meant we got very, very close to that £1 million (£863,000 if memory serves, and the full £1 million within six weeks). First, we divided the total to conquer it (see 'Divide and conquer' on page 5). How much could we get from grant-making trusts? How much from social groups? How much from a mailing? How much from our own staff and volunteers? How much from TV advertising? How much from events?

Second, and this applies to any amount of money you need to raise, we took pledges as well as cash. Every single one of those pledges came in and at higher sums than people had pledged. This is a clever move. Do not let your fundraising drag on forever at a public level; make the appeal short and sharp and in that narrow time frame ask for pledges to be made as well as donations given. Then let the fundraising carry on 'underground', as the pledges are realised and come in. Give yourself a month to raise the money in real cash or pledges but six months for those pledges to come in. It is so much easier to pledge something than to give it, and most people would be tormented by the idea of reneging on a pledge to a charity. Thus it is a fairly safe bet. Giving money seems much more possible and painless if you will not actually be handing over the cash for six months. (Why do you think you can always buy a sofa with no payment for a year?)

There were a few other lessons I learnt from that appeal.

- First, if you are going for a public appeal for anything, then limit the time you publicise your appeal. People will get bored with it quickly, even if you don't. Remember that the news is 'news' because it is new. The media and the public will soon lose interest if your appeal drags on forever.
- Second, if you are going public, do plenty of preparatory work beforehand, so that you are ready to make the most of your public phase.
- Third, if you need the media to raise awareness of the appeal, make sure you give them what they need. That is, well thought-out stories and events that can be effectively covered by the different media. Radio works well when the story or event, which focuses on people's lives and stories, creates pictures in the mind of the listener; TV, obviously, likes good visual images that are not static; and newspapers require the opposite.
- Fourth, remember that people like a challenge. You need something that distinguishes your appeal from the others. I found out (well after the event,

thankfully) that one of the local TV stations only covered the launch so that they would have library footage for their intended 'fundraising calamity' story when we would announce at the end of the appeal that we had raised £350.16 and ten knitted blankets. The target needs to challenge people so that there is a sense of progression and, in a funny way, danger. It gets the adrenaline running and gives a sense of momentum.

- Finally, if you go for a public appeal, try your very best to raise not quite enough. If this advice seems more than a little odd, then let me explain. Of all the people that you ask for money, how many will respond? 10%? 1%? 0.000001%? The greatest fundraising message you can have is 'We would have done it if only you had given.' Because of the £133,000 shortfall of our target for the hospice, that was the message that went out and that was why the rest of the money came in within six weeks.

The changing nature of stability

I prefer to remain in happy denial that I am inevitably getting older. Occasionally, though, something will cut through this denial and I will realise I am fast becoming that older person I judged so harshly in my twenties. In my team, we sometimes discuss significant cultural figures and events, and I have now learned that whenever I contribute to these conversations, I need to preface any comment with 'you might need to Google this' to give the younger members of the team an outside chance of knowing who or what I am talking about.

The team members have eclectic tastes, I think it is fair to say, and one of the topics of conversation was how we reacted when Take That split up. Some recounted their tears and anguish, some were indifferent, but we then discovered one member of the team hadn't even been born when this seismic event happened. That really makes you feel old, when someone you are talking to about an epoch-defining event wasn't even born in the epoch you are discussing.

As I try and age gracefully, I think one of the perks is to talk about how things were then and how they are now. It's not true that I grew a beard solely so I could stroke it while thinking ruminatively, but it is a definite plus of having one.

One of the things that has caused me much ruminative beard stroking is the changing nature of organisational stability. The first fundraising course I studied had an organisation illustrated in the shape of a Greek temple. It had solid foundations of sensibly sized reserves, historical performance, good marketing and PR, then different pillars of funding (public sector, individuals, community and trusts) that were all the same size so the pediment (or roof) of charity activity could be balanced securely and not too dependent on any one funding source. Looking back now, it seems almost quaint as a concept. The idea is great, but is that analogy the reality for most organisations now? I think not.

This is not to say that stability is not important; organisations need it as much now as ever. In fact, more so as we adjust to the colossal shocks and turbulence of a global pandemic, which is unlikely to be the last one we will need to live through. The challenge is finding that stability when everything seems to be constantly shifting.

If stability is desirable, but not achievable through the old models, then we need to reimagine how it could work. The closest analogy to stability in this new world order that I can offer is that of a surfer. To remain stable on a surfboard is immensely challenging, but it is essential to actually staying on the stupid thing (possibly venting a bit too much here). To achieve stability you need to be constantly assessing the environment, seeing where challenges will come from and spotting where opportunities are emerging. You need to be constantly shifting position and be ready to change direction as soon as you see things change but, critically, you need to keep moving forward. To switch our means of transportation metaphor from surfing to cycling, we need to live by the Einstein quote, which goes something along the lines of: 'Life is like riding a bicycle. In order to keep your balance, you must keep moving.' In other words, to be stable in this world is exactly the opposite of the temple model. Not necessarily because the model is wrong, but because reality shifts constantly and so our thinking must too.

On a management course I did when I was fresh out of college, the trainer talked of the importance of 'environment scanning' which, in those days, basically meant reading newspapers. It was a management task I found easier than others. But if the need for environment scanning was big then, it is enormously important now. A major factor in an organisation's success is its ability to spot developing trends and then use digital communications to engage with potential audiences. Digital communication has undoubtedly been one of the most profound changes and opportunities that have emerged since this book was initially written back in 2007. It amazes me to think the first edition of this book was written before Twitter (or whatever it is now called), Instagram and other social media became omnipresent. Digital communication has presented charities with enormous possibilities that previously did not exist in terms of ability to reach potential supporters, to communicate quickly, to control the narrative and to communicate in a professional, high-quality and impactful way.

But as digital communication has developed, it has got harder and harder to grab people's attention and to seize opportunities. Getting noticed requires an acute understanding of changing interests and issues. Which brings us back to surfing and the changing nature of stability and away from the temple building. We've moved from the solidity of land to the fluctuating adrenaline-rush of the sea, and acknowledging this reality is key to providing the stability every organisation needs.

The porcupine principle

The film *Edward Scissorhands* has, as its central character, a humanoid that is invented by a mad professor. The professor has almost completed his work, but his invention has scissors where his hands should be. Through a freak accident, Edward is made alive and so lives with scissors for hands. He then finds that he cannot express love and affection without harming people with his 'scissorhands'. It is a powerful allegory of damaged humanity and also a contemporary take on an old German fable that is the porcupine principle. In the fable, it is a cold winter, and a clan of porcupines decides to huddle together for warmth. Unfortunately, when they snuggled close to each other, they hurt each other with their spikes, so they withdrew from each other and grew cold again. Then they worked out that, if they were careful, they could stand just close enough to each other to keep the cold out but not so close that they spiked each other. This distance they called decency and good manners.

It would never harm your fundraising if you gave it the porcupine-principle test. If you are giving a talk, writing an article or having a conversation, are your supporters metaphorically freezing cold or reeling from being poked in the eye? The varying distance is dependent upon how well you manage to communicate the emotional consequences of the injustice you are trying to address, while at the same time not traumatising or manipulating the supporters.

Depending on the cause, it can be very hard to get this right.

One way of getting it right is to ask the question 'How would this make my grandmother feel?' A classic fundraising mistake is to ignore the fact that supporters are not the same age as you are. They will have different interests, use different idioms and phrases, and have different outlooks. Therefore, if you communicate in a way that you find comfortable, it is almost inevitable that some will not find it comfortable at all. When I started out in the fundraising world, it was still true for many charities that their average supporter has lived through at least one world war. As a truly marvellous 92-year-old supporter of a charity told me many years ago, 'We didn't have counselling, we just got on with it.' The reaction to emotional distress was not to peer endlessly into it, but to 'get on with it'. Endless recycling of angst and trauma through gut-wrenching case studies did not go down well with that supporter at least.

It is also easy to overplay the emotions, because you get wrapped up in your charity to the point where you become immune to the drama unfolding before you. As a consequence, you tend to raise the stakes, so you write and say things which you find shocking. What you find shocking can cause a heart attack for those who are not as aware of the cause.

If you really want to make sure that your message obeys the porcupine principle, get some of your supporters to look at it before you use it. Some people do not like criticising a charity, so choose your focus group with care, because you need them to be critical if your message is really going to hit home. If you go to the trouble of getting your focus group together, do not limit your research to just your message but ask them what they think about your whole fundraising programme too. It could be very illuminating.

Your fundraising message should not traumatise people, but at the same time it should not leave them cold either. My heart always sinks when I hear people talk about their charity, or when I read their publicity, and it starts with 'The charity was founded in the year x.' That is not cold, it is freezing cold. It is just as bad to roll out statistics as a means of describing why you are important. Remember: you need to show people the consequences of your actions, not the actions themselves.

When I was CEO of a special needs charity, I could have described it as 'a school that was founded in 1826 for deaf children in the southwest of England'. Is that why it was important? I could have described it as running a residential school and college for deaf children aged 5–22. Is that why it was important? I could have described it as a charity employing over one hundred people and having a turnover in excess of £3 million. Is that why it was important? Or I could have said that it existed to enable deaf children to acquire a language, to achieve independence, to develop socially and emotionally, and to excel educationally. How can that not be important? I could have said that we wanted deaf people to be valued by themselves and their society, to be confident, well educated, independent and able to communicate, and to have good and appropriate employment and housing. How can that not be important? And I could have done this best by enabling our students to communicate what a difference we had made for them or, even better, by letting the supporters see for themselves.

When I showed people around the school, they entered a different world. When we sat down in the school canteen, we soon realised that we were lost, surrounded in a sea of sign language that we could not understand. Many found it a distressing experience; they did not realise what a lonely and isolating experience it can be not to be able to communicate with those around you.

This is something our students experienced every day in the 'hearing world'. If I wanted to poke our visitors in the eye, I would leave them alone in the canteen for half an hour and let the isolation swamp them. If I wanted to freeze them, I would never let them see this. But if I wanted to abide by the porcupine principle, I would sit with them in the canteen and have an interpreter with me.

Every charity I have worked for has an equivalent challenge when communicating what it does. As an aside, every charity I have worked for also believes it is the only charity that the general public does not understand. But the very nature of our non-profit business means that it is a mystery to many people. Our job as fundraisers is to demystify it. When I worked in a youth centre in south-east London, I could have poked the supporters in the eye by asking them to walk through the local estates any evening with a youth worker. Alternatively, I could have frozen them by not letting them see anything other than my office. or perhaps by letting them see some of the 'nice' primary school-age children's activities. Or I could have given them a 'minder' and let them sit in on a session on our site and the neighbouring green with some of the local teenagers.

Every charity will have an equivalent scenario, so think through how you can make your charity come alive for a supporter and then test your ideas against the porcupine principle.

Hidden treasure

When my soul was in the lost and found, you came along to claim it.

Gerry Goffin and Carole King,
'You Make Me Feel (Like a Natural Woman)'

One of the reasons that charities are fabulous is because they are full of people, and people are, in their own way, fabulous. Just about everyone has genuinely extraordinary tales to tell. It might be something that happened to them or somebody they know, or something they have done. We do not spend anywhere near enough time finding out about the remarkable people in our midst, and we certainly do not spend enough time thinking of ourselves as remarkable. Yet we are, in so many ways; we just forget about it or else our familiarity with our being remarkable breeds contempt for it.

When I was a child, I absolutely idolised a footballer by the name of John Byrne. He played for the paragon of professional football, York City FC. He was part of the championship winning side (fourth division) in the 1980s, and he lived on my road. He lived on my road! A footballing god was a mere hop, skip and a jump away.

As I write, York City are languishing in mid-table mediocrity of the National League, one hugely optimistic promotion away from what was the fourth division, which was previously named the third division, which later became the second division (if you do not know why, it takes too long to explain). Back in the 1980s, things were just about as bleak, except York were bumping along at the bottom of the fourth division, and that was as bad as it could get because there was no relegation in those days. Anyway, a new manager called Dennis Smith arrived and was observing a training session. He saw, amidst this struggling squad of players, an exceptional talent. He asked a long-serving staff member who that person was, and the reply went something like 'That's John Byrne, we've been trying to get rid of him for a while but we haven't had much interest.' The new manager promptly put John Byrne in the first team, and he and the team never looked back (well, not for a few seasons anyway). Championships were won, Arsenal were beaten in the FA cup (I was there!) and Liverpool could only draw with us in the FA cup soon afterwards – heady days.

My point is that treasure is everywhere; you have just got to look for it. Dennis Smith saw it in that training session. A vital part of being a fundraiser is to discover the hidden treasure within your charity. The treasure will take many forms, but it will be there (unless you are very unlucky). The treasure might be people, contacts or assets.

People

It is remarkable how many skills and interests lie dormant within any organisation. Those skills and interests can be invaluable in organising fundraising events and appeals. You can only find out about them by getting to know the people outside a work environment. Ordinarily, people will be delighted to be asked to exercise them for a fundraising campaign, you just have to ask them to do something that they feel confident about and enjoy doing. Asking a kite surfer to do face painting will elicit a very different response from asking them to give free kite-surfing lessons.

Contacts

Start with the assumption that every single person connected with your charity will know someone else who could be valuable to you. The snag is that the person may not know exactly who is valuable – or why – but, to be honest, that hardly matters. Just get them talking about who they know, and you can make the connections. I have often wondered whether the really whizzy fundraising departments use those glass notice boards like the ones in TV detective series. They always have grisly pictures of dead people and arrows pointing to bubbles with names in them, or to other photos of people or places. Heaven only knows what those boards are for (except they do make great TV), but I presume it is all about trying to find connections, and so it should be as useful to fundraisers as to detectives (and it is so much jollier to be trying to find a multi-millionaire rather than a murderer).

When I was running the 'Thanks a million' appeal (see page 39) at St Luke's Hospice in Plymouth, I met all the members of the appeal committee and asked them how they believed they were to contribute to the appeal. Without exception, they all said the one thing they would not do was ask anyone for money. That was, they said, quite clearly my job. When I tried to get some leads from their personal address books, they were even more horrified than when I asked them to actually raise money. Handing over their contacts would be an unforgivable social *faux pas*; their friends would simply never forgive them for letting a fundraiser loose on them. When trying to raise a lot of money, this was not a promising start. However, all ended well.

We needed to raise another £50,000 to meet the £1million target for this fundraising appeal to redevelop our hospice. The chair of our appeal, a truly delightful man who had, at the start of the appeal, been the most horrified at the idea of asking anyone for anything, brought in that last £50,000. He did it in the most marvellous style. He rang up a friend of a friend and said words to the effect of 'You don't know me. I'm the chair of the appeal for a local hospice. We need £50,000, and I hear you are a very generous man.' The cheque came that afternoon. (Rather disappointingly, it was just a normal cheque, written in Biro! I thought a £50,000 cheque should at least be on some classy vellum paper and clearly written with a quill.) The donor had done something absolutely remarkable, but so had my chair – and I do not know of whom I was more proud.

Assets

This deserves a book all of its own, and past projects (like the sustainable funding project by the National Council of Voluntary Organisations) have looked at this in much more depth. Suffice it to say that many charities have something that could be very valuable to others, but they just have not seen it in that way before. Do you have an expertise that others would pay to access through training? Do you have spare rooms that you could rent out? Do you have spare capacity within your admin team that you could subcontract to another organisation? Would a company pay good money to be associated with your fundraising or delivery of services through sponsorship? Have you got a way of working or an idea that is not only very valuable to you but could also be used by others through a form of licensing agreement?

Later on during my time at St Luke's, the fundraising team created a 'forget-me-not' garden. It is a digression, but this is a great example of how fundraisers can make the charity better at its core business. Anyway, the garden was just beyond the car park, past the ropey looking large shed and by the compost heap. It does not sound promising, does it? But we worked out that if you hacked back the overgrown bushes, you had majestic views out to the sea. And, because the land was so steep, you could add water to the garden and create a remembrance pool at the bottom. A local gardening firm came up with an inspired design, and so the garden was created, with the hospice offering to engrave pebbles with the names of loved ones, which the relatives could then place in the pool. Relatives come back year after year. It has been hugely beneficial to many people, despite being beyond the car park, past the ropey looking large shed and by the compost heap. What have you got that could do the same?

Hidden treasure is everywhere, waiting to be found, so put this book down and go and find it.

How much did your house cost?

One of the essentials of fundraising success is being pragmatic. We might want the world to be a certain way, but it isn't. And if we pretend that it is, we are in trouble. For example, just because we are comfortable doing some things, that does not mean that everyone is. This is particularly important for charities and fundraising. We are often slightly bonkers about our cause, for all manner of reasons, and so it is easy to forget that most people simply are not moved in the same way. We may think that there is no more worthy thing than our charity, we may happily talk about how much we give and why, but that does not mean others want to do the same. So, do not try to change the DNA of your potential donors by forcing them to talk about things that they absolutely do not want to talk about. Like money.

Remember that, as a fundraiser, you are not here to change the world; you are here to enable your cause to prosper within it. I am sorry to be so brutal, but it is true. You should not confuse what your charity is doing with what your fundraising practice should be. While a charity itself is often changing the world, fundraisers have more functional aspirations (see 'Realpolitik' on page 97 for more on that). You are not here to convert people to the noble activity of donating to charities; you are here to find as many donors as possible for your charity at as low a cost as possible. The more you try to change people's behaviour at the same time as raising money, the less money you will get. Your job is absolutely not to get your donors to adopt your views, opinions and mindset; your job is to get inside their heads, so that you see how giving to your cause can fit seamlessly within their world. You may be happy talking about what you give to a cause, but I know that most people are not.

If your eyes have not glazed over completely by this point, you may be struggling to reconcile this fact with other chapters that talk about the importance of being visionary, challenging the status quo, blue sky thinking, thinking outside the box, pushing the envelope and other tortuous management clichés. However, that points to another essential fundraising truth: fundraising, like life, is a paradox and a contradiction. It is best to be happy with the ambiguity that this creates rather than to fight it.

So, what are people like? Well, one of the things you can absolutely guarantee is that the overwhelming number of English people you will meet will hate, really hate, talking about money. If you want to know more about this, then do read Kate Fox's book, *Watching the English: The Hidden Rules of English Behaviour*, which is simply marvellous.

I know it is a sweeping generalisation (although if you are going to generalise, you may as well sweep with it), but many people, English people particularly, do not like talking about money. Just picture this scene: you are at a party and someone mentions that they have bought a new house. What kinds of questions will be asked? How many bedrooms? Has it a garage? How many toilets/bathrooms? Does it have a kitchen diner/lounge diner/diner diner? How big is the garden? What are the neighbours like? What area is it in? What condition is the house in? What rooms will be changed? One question that will certainly not be asked is: how much did it cost? This is absurd. It is fairly obvious that this is a big part of the equation, but it is rarely, if ever, asked.

As someone who has to talk to people about something that practically no one wants to talk about, you have a significant challenge on your hands. How do you ask people for money? Be cunning. If you ask someone directly, in public, for money, they will hate you for it. They may give you money once, in order to try to minimise the embarrassment, but they will not forgive you for jabbing them so hard where it psychologically hurts. If you only want money from them once, then I suppose you have nothing to lose, but that rationale is mostly used by double-glazing salespeople. I'll leave you to ponder the implications of that sentence.

The best way of asking people for money is by not asking them for money (of course!). That does not mean that they are not challenged to give, but you do it in a way that does not mention the words 'you', 'give' and 'money' within the same sentence. So, as a warm-up, you talk about what the issue is that you are addressing, why it is important, why it needs charitable support, what a difference that support will make and ways that people can give. Then (and this is pushing it a bit, but I have not had any negative response to this so far), you give some examples of what is needed in order for the money to be raised. For example, if 10 people give £10 a month, and 20 people give £5 a month, then we'll have the funding we need to start our new project.

Next, and this is really important, you make it quite clear that you need people to think and decide now. They do not have to talk about it publicly and they do not need to enter group discussions, but they must decide now or (if they must have time to think about it) they might at least give you permission to contact them at a later date to remind them. The most popular reason for not giving money is because people forget. That is why deciding there and then is great, but if it feels too much like high-pressure sales tactics, then make sure you have created the mechanism for a follow-up conversation. However it goes, get it down in writing.

If you really want to avoid the high-pressure stuff, then I would recommend that you ask someone who is already a giver to explain why they give. If you are officially representing a charity, whether you are paid or unpaid, you automatically create a certain distance between you and your potential supporter. They do not see you as 'one of us' but 'one of them'. You are someone who has a vested interest, either financial or psychological, in getting them to part with money. Therefore, get someone who is like them to ask them to do what they do. It is neat and it works.

One final pointer, and it is implied above: when asking for money, always, always make the amount seem as palatable as possible. If you asked anyone for £120, they would think twice. They are much more likely to say yes if you ask for £10 now and then ask them to give £10 every month for the next eleven months. Giving at this level becomes more manageable for the donor, and every bit as valuable for the charity. Standing orders or direct debits are an invaluable gift to fundraisers. They enable big-sounding amounts of money to be broken down into manageable chunks. They are administratively easy, and, once set up, they become an accepted way of life to the donor – something that is absorbed into their monthly outgoings. This aspect of fundraising may not seem particularly idealistic, but it is pragmatic. And, in fundraising, pragmatism is king.

'From this distance they couldn't hit an ele...'

One of my lifetime ambitions is to write a book based on people's last words. It is a good indication of a warped mind, I freely admit, but I think it would make a corking read. What do you think yours would be? What would you like them to be? My suspicion is that General John Sedgwick did not anticipate that his last words would be 'from this distance they couldn't hit an ele...'. He was responding to the increasingly alarmed requests of his troops to open fire on the rapidly advancing enemy in the American Civil War. His logic, reasonably sound, was that if they were too far away, then the bullets would just be wasted, as they had little chance of hitting the intended target. Better to save them for when they could actually do the job they were meant for. Unfortunately for him, the enemy was a far better judge of distance than he was.

Being able to judge distance is an essential part of being a fundraiser. If you get a group of people together and tell them they must raise, say, £1,000, one of the first ideas that people normally come up with is writing to companies, particularly local retailers for some reason. It is part of our knee-jerk reaction to having to ask people for money – a perfectly sensible way of trying to avoid the embarrassment of actually talking about money face to face. Unfortunately, indiscriminately bombarding high-street businesses with a request rarely works. Any reasonably sized company will get stacks of these requests every week, and the vast majority will be unsuccessful.

There are many reasons why this rarely works. Partly, it is because companies genuinely do not have the money; the high street particularly is a brutal place to try and make any kind of money. Partly, it is because they do not want to be seen to be encouraging these kinds of requests. Partly, it is because they have not really thought through the idea of charitable giving as part of their *raison d'être*. Back in the day, I was chatting to a senior partner in a very large law firm, who admitted that 'social responsibility' was a bit odd for them, frankly, and they couldn't see how it fitted. I will resist the obvious jokes about solicitors here. It's true that generally companies are more savvy about these things than they used to be, but it is still often peripheral to the activities and workings of the company.

However, the big reason why writing to companies does not work is because it takes much more than this to persuade people to hand money over. Such an approach presumes that office staff in large companies are sitting at their desks debating among themselves as to whom they could go and give money to. Of course life is not like this. If they are debating anything, they are debating who is going to be evicted from I'm a Celebrity. If people don't have a giving reflex, and they normally don't, then giving is a predetermined action, and furthermore a predetermined action they would prefer not to make.

A written communication (be it letter, email or whatever) is far too removed and distant; the communication needs to be much closer in order to work. A good rule of thumb is never to ask for money until you can see the whites of the person's eyes. That is not always possible, but it should be in most cases. Giving is a simple process made complex by our confused morality. It is a subject we instinctively shun. As fundraisers, we need to find a way to reassure people, to enable them to overcome their natural reticence to think on these things. That is very difficult to do by letter and much easier when face to face.

This reality conforms to the eternal truth that the harder something is, the more effective it will be. Writing indiscriminately to any company you can think of asking them for money is like chucking a pot of paint on a wall and expecting it to look as if it has been professionally decorated. It would be great if decorating really were this easy, but it's not, and neither is fundraising. Fundraising takes time and care – just like decorating does – and, to stretch the metaphor a bit, it can't be done easily at a distance.

Asking someone for money when they are standing in front of you, or indeed sitting, costs a lot of emotional energy and courage. You are behaving atypically, after all, but then it is much more likely to work. Only by 'whites of their eyes' fundraising do you pick up on all that non-verbal stuff that is so important when shaping your request. If they are in front of you, people do not have to tell you to get lost for you to realise that they do not like the cut of your jib. The avoidance of eye contact, the crossed arms or legs (or both), the smack on the head – all these are subtle ways of telling you that you are going about it the wrong way. This gives you a chance to change tack, to back off and to explain things in a different way. It also (very importantly) gives you the chance to show that this really matters to you, and people love that. People want to be inspired, to be part of something big, and the best way of doing that is by telling them.

If the whole idea makes you squeamish, I have a suggestion for you. Do not see your job as fund*raising*, but as fund*asking*. You are not forcing anyone to do anything but just asking them whether they would. As you know, to ask for something is not the same thing as to demand something. If you *demand* something, there is normally a lot of shouting, perhaps even the stamping of feet, and much manipulation and bullying, often with some form of threat thrown in. Some people do fundraise in this way, regrettably. However, if you *ask* for something, it tends to be asked in a gentle tone; it is a request that does give the opportunity for a yes or a no answer, and it is normally sprinkled with politeness. Is that not a more comfortable prospect? My favourite line is to say something like 'In order to fund our [fill in your project details here], I need to find 20 people to give £5 a month and I wondered whether you might be one of them? If you can't help, that's absolutely fine, but I hope you don't mind my asking. Thanks.' Better?

The map is not the territory

If you were to think of two diametrically opposite roles, I think astronaut and fundraiser would be right up there. Although I guess both have work overalls, if you count the fancy dress outfits we so often seem to end up wearing for fundraising events as work overalls. My favourite was dressing up as a chicken for a duck race. (Dear readers, the explanation of this would be too tortuous to recount here so I beg to be excused.)

This makes the learning on fundraising in the astronaut Chris Hadfield's book *An Astronaut's Guide to Life on Earth* quite surprising. It is a great read, providing an insight into a job that is literally otherworldly to mine. He writes a lot about planning and the importance of it to an astronaut, so, I guess, he may not be that impressed to be name-checked in a chapter which argues how unimportant planning is.

Where I think he, and Alfred Korzybski (who coined the phrase that I've tweaked in the title), would agree is that what we plan to do and what happens are rarely the same thing. Hadfield describes a simulation exercise to repair a broken satellite in space that was based on false assumptions. The exercise team had tested the procedure endlessly on the ground, where they had some nifty kit to simulate the weightlessness of space. Except, as they discovered too late, it didn't replicate the conditions in space exactly, and, as a result, what worked in the simulator didn't work in space. If your plan has similarly false assumptions, then there is a danger you will, as Chris Hadfield says, draw 'the wrong, perfectly polished conclusions' too. And that's my point about planning and its limitations. The plan depends on accurate assumptions about what will happen, and that is becoming ever more difficult. I have produced some plans in my time that had 'perfectly polished conclusions' that were wrong. The plan (or map) looked beautiful, but it failed to anticipate the way the territory changed, or did not understand the territory accurately enough.

It is not that planning is wrong, just that, in times of turbulence, it is more challenging and harder to get it right, and so we need to keep re-checking that the assumptions that underpin our plan are right. It is making sure we have the meerkat instinct, regularly stopping to look to the horizon to see new dangers and opportunities. Either that or, if this all sounds too much like hard work, then try the simpler approach and follow the maxim that if you want to be sure of hitting the target, shoot first and then call whatever you hit the target.

Reading Hadfield's book, I was surprised to discover that some astronauts never actually get to go into space. They spend their entire lives not doing what people understandably think of as their job. Politics, finance, weather, disasters, ill health and other factors can all conspire to keep some astronauts literally grounded. This reality requires an enviable mindset for Hadfield. 'Ultimately, I don't determine whether I arrive at the desired professional destination. Too many variables are out of my control. There's really just one thing I can control: my attitude during the journey...'

Hadfield shows how critical it is that we manage our expectations and not use our lack of control as an excuse for giving up. It is perfectly possible, and a good mindset, to strive for something remarkable, acknowledging that whether we achieve it or not depends on many factors we cannot control.

So maybe our jobs are not so different after all. Working in the charity sector is all about striving for something remarkable, and often about working in a hostile, complex and ever-changing environment. It is also a feature of a fundraiser's life that so many things which we cannot control can influence the extent to which we are successful at fundraising. And if our jobs are more similar than I thought, maybe it also makes sense to endeavour to adopt the same mindset too and to focus on controlling our attitude along the fundraising journey we are on.

This links to another favourite quote from Hadfield about preparing not planning: 'The truth is that nothing went as we'd planned, but everything was within the scope of what we prepared for.' In a volatile and uncertain world, this surely is key – however much you may believe in the effectiveness or accuracy of planning, being prepared for what comes your way is fundamental to fundraising success.

Jackanory, tell me a story

The title of this chapter probably only makes sense if you were at primary school in the 1980s or before. If you were, then right now you probably are bathing in the sentimental glow of time spent watching an incredible roll call of acting talent reading a favourite story. Actors reading a story to camera – was that it? Well, yup, pretty much. Sometimes they would change the armchair they sat in, but that was about all. It was the perfect example of the compelling power of simply telling a story.

When I am giving talks on fundraising, there are normally two parts of those talks that people prefer over the rest. Ironically, neither of them is about fundraising. The first is the five essential truths of male initiation ceremonies ('The five essential truths' on page 154) and the second is the story of Larry Walters.

The story of Larry Walters is a great illustration of how to communicate a fundraising message. Fundraising is about people helping people. When you are talking about your cause, therefore, do not talk about the mechanics, the equipment, the buildings, the politics or the statistics; talk instead about people. Even better, get the people themselves to talk. There is absolutely nothing as powerful as someone telling you their story, of how their life has been changed through the work that you do.

An example of this, I remember, was when I visited a women's refuge and listened to the story of one of the residents. I met her a few decades ago now, but I can still remember what she said. She said that her husband first hit her on her wedding night and how, after he did that, she threw her wedding ring into the fire. I also remember a different occasion when I read a letter from a relative of a hospice patient in which she wrote 'St Luke's is such a beautiful place, filled with such beautiful people. I'm sure that when my Dad reached heaven he would hardly have noticed the difference.' I also remember I heard a huge lad, with hands the size of shovels, telling me how he was bullied at school because he was deaf and how the other pupils wouldn't give him his football back. Writing about these conversations now upsets me because they provide a window into the lives of those who are suffering. Stories move us in a way that nothing else does.

There are many theories as to why we are so interested in each other. One of the more plausible ones is that, as relatively weedy animals, we needed to stick together in order to survive in prehistoric times. If you were rejected and then ejected from your clan, you were as good as dead. Our ancestors realised that they needed to make sure that they were always in the 'in' crowd, could identify who the powerful ones were and were able to ensure that they were always on the right side. They did that by listening and talking to others about others, and that instinct, over a few millennia, turned into *Heat* magazine.

Whatever the reason, there is nothing like a story to attract people's attention, and there are not many better than the story about Larry Walters. He, to my knowledge, did not raise a penny for good causes through his exploits. However, his story is a truly inspiring and hilarious one and he embodies many of the really excellent qualities that fundraisers need.

Larry Walters had always wanted to fly. He used to sit in his garden chair in the back yard of his Los Angeles home and watch the planes fly overhead on their way to the airport. He was neither rich nor bright enough to become an airline pilot, but why should that stop him? He got together a parachute, a citizens band radio, a six-pack of beer, some peanut-butter sandwiches, a ball-bearing gun, a flashlight, extra batteries and an altimeter. The final pieces of the flying jigsaw were 45 helium-filled weather balloons.

His preferred mode of transport was his garden chair so he tied the balloons to them. He thought that the balloons would take the chair up a few hundred feet so that he could look down over his neighbourhood, eat a few sandwiches, drink a few beers and then, when he was bored, he would pop a few of the balloons with the ball-bearing gun and gradually ease back down to earth.

The reality was that, when he untethered the garden chair, he rose at 1,000 feet a minute and eventually settled at 16,000 feet (3 miles up). We know it was 16,000 feet because he was at the same height as the airplanes circling the airport before landing. He ascended so fast that his glasses fell off (bad news) and he dropped the ball-bearing gun (very bad news).

He drifted for an age before crashing into power lines, blacking out a neighbourhood, but he miraculously survived. In my mind, this makes him a hero. Superb planning, creativity, determination, ingenuity, bravery, success and, boy, did he know how to make a media story. With the benefit of hindsight he was perhaps a bit over the top with the number of balloons but, that apart, he did a sparkling job. Sadly, others did not agree and he was fined $1,500 for 'operating a civil aircraft for which there is not currently in effect an airworthiness certificate' and for being in airport space and not contacting the control tower. A local bureaucrat rather marvellously said that 'We know he broke some part of the Federal Aviation Act and, as soon as we decide which part it is, some type of charge will be filed.

If he had a pilot's license, we'd suspend that. But he doesn't.' When asked why he did it, he said 'It was something I had to do. I had this dream for 20 years, and if I hadn't done it, I would have ended up in the funny farm.' Fundraising is about overcoming insurmountable odds. This story is a fantastic inspiration not to be constrained by a 'safety first' mindset but to think in a different and creative way. When I talk about Larry Walters, I could choose instead to list his attributes and talk about how important they are. But it would be boring and people would not remember. When you are planning your fundraising, remember the example of Larry Walters. Also, when you are talking about your charity, remember the fact that you remember Larry Walters because you heard a story about him, and make sure you tell a story too.

Charisma, passion, leadership and illusion

'Well, you see, the thing is, and I do not mean to be a bind, but I just wonder whether you wouldn't mind, which I am sure you wouldn't because you're such a star, helping perhaps with a little idea that I've got, I mean we've got, that kind of tries to, well, you know perhaps raise a bit, well at least try and raise a bit, of, err, money, but it probably won't because I'm totally hopeless, but, well, you might be able to kind of rescue my useless efforts and perhaps prevent it from being a total disaster if you would well, help, or at least think about helping, even though to be honest it probably won't do much good, and they probably wouldn't even notice if we did anything or not, and I'm sure you've got a million things better to do with your time, and I feel really bad for even taking up your time by asking you, and poor old you having to listen to me prattle on when you know you could be doing something useful with your time...'

All right, it is a bit of an exaggeration, but as exaggerations go it is not that much of one. Fundraising does not work if you raise obfuscation to an art form. Fundraising needs to be focused, with a clear sense of direction and purpose. This is true when you are asking people for money and even more so when you are asking people to ask other people for money. For fundraising to work it needs leadership. It needs someone to say 'We're going to do this, and raise this much, by this date.' I know it might not sit comfortably with some, but we are not all leaders and many people want to be led by someone else. They also want to know that what they are doing is important, significant even, and that it will make some meaningful difference. This requires leadership, and if you have not got it, then you really, really need to find someone within your fundraising team or group who has.

Leaders need to be good not only at giving attainable targets but also at linking them with the impact that those targets will make on the beneficiaries of your charity. They need to be able to explain why it is crucial that the money is raised and why each person is doing something incredibly important to enable that target to be reached. I would argue that they also need to exude a sense of calm authority, of being in control and of knowing with a deep and profound assurance that whatever they are doing will succeed. This is very important. It is even more important to have this aura when it has no basis in fact.

I know this is somewhat dubious morally, but fundraising is to a certain extent a conjuring trick. It is all about getting people to commit themselves, whether to time or money. However, people will often only commit themselves to something they are sure will succeed. Fundraising can be compared to the way people sit in any kind of gathering – no one wants to be in front, everybody wants to sit anonymously at the back (churches are particularly known for it). There are times when you are not sure whether the fundraising really is worth the effort, because sufficient funds might not be raised, but if you show your uncertainties, your efforts are guaranteed to fail. It is an archetypal self-fulfilling prophecy.

Sometimes you may also be uncertain whether the money really needs to be raised at all. The better you get to know your charity, the better you will understand what it does poorly as well as what it does well. Charities are no different from other organisations. They are just as good at wasting money on half-baked and poorly thought-through projects. Hearing about those cock-ups, though, does not make for a motivational fundraising speech.

I was once sent a letter asking whether I wished to be taken out in a boat on to the deep blue sea, where I would be thrown overboard and rescued by a 14-stone dog. Forgive me if I am wrong, but I would want some pretty good assurance that being slobbered over by an overgrown St Bernard would give any kind of significant benefit to the charity's beneficiaries. I would not be motivated to do it by the above suggestion, or by someone who is heard whinging about the waste of money spent on the charity's new offices.

I digress. Good fundraising is to a certain extent an illusion. Sometimes it is about having a calm assured exterior when mentally you are actually looking frantically for the metaphorical fire exits. If someone has to raise £2,000 before they go on their beloved sponsored dog-sled trek, there are only two weeks to go and they have only raised £200, they do not want you saying 'Yup, love, the game's up.' They want you to say 'Of course you'll do it, money always comes in at the last moment, you've raised more than I did at the same point last year.' and so on. It may or may not be strictly true, but there is only one response that offers a chance of the money coming in. Experienced and good fundraisers will tell you, if they are honest, that there are numerous times like this.

This relates to an instinctive ability to appear interested in things that bore you rigid. The positive spin is to say you are a social chameleon, able to be fascinated by all manner of interests, hobbies and opinions. The negative spin is that you are being insincere, feigning interest in whatever subject a funder is fascinated by. I have had long conversations with people about undeniably the most boring pastime in the world – golf – and I do not think they've twigged my real opinion about it. I have chortled along to people making rude comments about the greatest football team in the world – Spurs – without giving my allegiance away. These are relatively trivial, and tolerating conversations or opinions that you may find dull or disagree with is hardly a unique experience of fundraising in the world of work. But to be able to tolerate interests and views that are different to yours can be a key part of building the relationships that fundraising needs. There are clearly lines that should not be crossed in terms of the behaviour and comments of those who may support your cause, and to be clear I am not talking about this here. This is about accepting the reality that, for example, if golf days are a key part of your charity's fundraising, and you don't like golf, then it is prudent to not draw attention to that fact at the golf days you attend.

So, fundraising can be something of a moral quagmire. It can sometimes be about leading when you are not convinced about what you are doing or why, whether your cause deserves it or whether you will get there. It can be about telling people you are sure they are being good fundraisers when you haven't seen much evidence to date. Or engaging in conversations on subjects which you have no interest in. I can't see why more people aren't doing it.

Assessing the risks of risk assessments

> *Life has become safer as human society has experimented… Safety was not something that could be acquired just by wanting it. Those who propose to avoid risks and gain safety will invariably find that what they acquire instead are obsessions.*
>
> Frank Furedi, sociologist

This chapter might turn into a bit of a rant against modern life, and I will try to avoid that. However, judging by the way some people live their lives, we exist on the brink of wholesale anarchy and chaos. It is one of those bizarre things about our modern society that, while we live far safer and healthier lives than we have ever done before, our perception is exactly the reverse. I think our sensitivities have become heightened to anything that is out of the ordinary, was not predicted, or cannot be quantified and measured. As life has become safer, we have become less equipped to cope with things going wrong. As a result, the impact of things going wrong is all the greater, despite the fact that the thing going wrong may be relatively minor in itself.

This showed itself most clearly in the hospice I worked in. Death is perhaps the ultimate and most brutal lesson to us in that we are not in control; not half as much as we think we are, anyway. When it comes to the really big things (health, love, life, relationships, financial security), we are actually quite powerless. But we prefer to think that we are not, that in fact our actions dictate our well-being and that safety is something we can acquire in the way we acquire a new TV.

I do believe we are becoming ever more timid and frightened about engaging with things that are not familiar, because we wrongly think this will keep us safe. Paradoxically, as we observe society in its ever greater complexity and variety, we are becoming less likely to engage with it. This social phenomenon has an impact on fundraising too. One of the difficulties of fundraising is that, in order to capture the imagination, it often has to be doing something new. However, something new inevitably carries greater risks than something well known, so the pressure is always to stick with the tried and tested. Thus, fundraising ideas that start off as totally off the wall – a sponsored 'let's build a two-storey house out of chocolate rolls' – turns into a sponsored silence before you can say 'risk assessment'.

Risk assessments, whatever their blessings may be, are in some ways the curse of modern fundraising. The people who have the ultimate say are often the people who couldn't see a good fundraising idea if it came up and slapped them around the face (which it wouldn't be allowed to do, of course, because of the potential risk of physical harm to the person). It is so much easier to say why something will not work rather than how it will: 'taking to pieces is the trade of those who cannot construct', as Ralph Waldo Emerson put it so beautifully. There are literally thousands of people out there who exist to tell you why you cannot do something and far fewer who can actually create something original and dynamic.

Having watched my children stagger and crash through the toddler years, I think it is frankly a miracle that they have survived at all. Danger is everywhere, and so we try to control it, but that in turn just makes children more creative in seeking danger. Risk is an inherent part of life. Indeed, the taking of risk is, I would argue, one of the most effective ways of learning something. By taking us beyond that which is familiar, we learn far more about ourselves, our own resourcefulness and the world in which we live. The psychological straitjacket we live in can, ironically, cause us immense harm.

So, how do you preserve your risk-taking ethos? The first and most important part is that you must, in the initial stages of developing any fundraising idea, absolutely banish any criticism of the idea. Give the idea time to flourish and grow and to develop before it is critiqued. Most people have an instinctive reaction to something new that is one of wariness or even open hostility. The brain sends out a 'repel all boarders' instruction as the new idea tries to climb aboard, and the endorphins do a happy jig as they see the new idea sink like a stone. The idea needs to be protected from the risk assessors (there's an irony) until it has the strength to bat them off.

Second, do not instinctively believe someone who says something cannot be done. The assessment of risk is often a judgement or opinion about what is reasonable, yet opinions can often be offered as if they were absolute facts that are non-negotiable.

Third, be patient. Try little risks first and build up a good track record of successfully taking small risks that achieve good returns. People may not trust your idea but they may trust you, and if you have a good track record, they will be more likely to go with the idea.

Fourth, seek wise counsel from someone who knows you and/or knows fundraising. It is easy to get so wrapped up in a fundraising idea, we don't see the dangers of fundraising events or campaigns (whether of the risk to the people involved or the risk of not raising any money).

Finally, just go for it and make sure you learn from the experience and that it shapes the way you fundraise in the future. Always, always, always give time to reflect on your fundraising event or appeal very soon after it has finished, because that is when you are often at your most insightful. Reflect, and write it down. A personal favourite is to list the 'near hits'. People are attuned to writing down their 'near misses', when something almost went wrong, but they just got away with it. A 'near hit' is when something went OK but could have gone much better if they had just adapted it slightly; for example, the hot dog stand raised £50 but, as people would have paid another 50p per hot dog, it could have raised £100. Really good fundraisers are always restless, always looking to improve and always looking to challenge the way things have always been done.

Even a blind chicken finds some grain

Whatever else you do in fundraising, look busy. It does not really matter what kind of fundraising you do, just make sure you look busy doing it. I believe that a lot of the busyness in fundraising is there to mask a basic lack of confidence in the core business of raising funds. We are not really sure why people give us money. This means that we cannot control something we are supposed to be responsible for. You see this often in fundraising analysis. The need to know information that enables you to influence practice is almost secondary to the creation of a comforting theory that explains historical giving.

Community fundraising events can be the epitome of busy fundraising. I have been rebuked more than once when I have challenged an event organiser to show me any evidence to support their argument that their event has promoted legacy giving. I frequently hear this argument and I suspect it is in part because the legacy blanket is marvellous protection against the cruel, cold winds of analysis of your 'bang for your buck' fundraiser. The 'events lead to legacies' argument is the same as that of the German proverb that even a blind chicken finds some grain. If you peck around for long enough, however blindly, you will eventually find something. That does not mean that it is the best way for you to spend your time or your money, and a little critical thinking can save you much of both. I personally think it is morally indefensible to carry on spending valuable charity resources on a fundraising methodology which is less effective than another fundraising methodology. People give money to your cause in order to help those who benefit from your cause's work and not because they want to humour people who like one form of fundraising more than another.

Fundraising planning can sound terribly grandiose but it is not really. It is a fairly simple process of asking perfectly sensible questions like:

1. How much money do I need to raise?
2. What ways are there of raising the money?
3. Which raises the most money for the least expense?
4. What are the key tasks that need to be accomplished?
5. Who will do what and when?
6. What worked well, what didn't and what nearly worked well or nearly went wrong?

There is a tendency to rush headlong into fundraising activity, but it, like most things, benefits hugely from some time spent at the planning stage. As fundraisers, we have a serious responsibility to educate the public. Even if people do have higher aspirations for fundraising than just shaking a collecting tin, they normally go no further than thinking they could run a community event. I once had a charming letter from someone who said they would help to organise a fundraising event for my charity as long as we sorted out the venue, catering, entertainment, music and sold the tickets. Leaving aside what is left to organise after delegating all of that, I think the event idea was suggested because that is the default response to a fundraising challenge – 'let's organise an event'.

The fundraising in question was in order to acquire some nifty bit of IT for my school's children to use to help with their learning. The total needed was £2,000. Using our divide and conquer method (see page 5), that is four times £500. Could I persuade a local social group to raise £500? Or the local church? Could I give direct debit forms to any parents who wanted to contribute? Could I ask a grant-making trust for some of the money? Could the pupils raise some funds themselves? How about twisting the arm of one of my trustees to get their company to sponsor it? All of these ways are much more likely to raise the funds, and cost far less money and take fewer hours, than a fundraising event. A little time and thought at the beginning of the process can save an age of work, stress and money later on.

It is our job as fundraisers to point this out, to show people a different way. People's instincts are very often cautious and unoriginal. They fall back on what they have seen before rather than thinking of something new. They need to be inspired to think differently and that is what we are here to do. It does not need to be hugely complicated. The Parent Teacher Friends Association of my local school had to organise the school summer fête. The usual half-dozen suspects were anticipating being lumbered with organising the whole thing. However, one of the committee members came up with a cunning plan. Rather than ask for volunteers for the whole fête, she created two shifts so that people could still enjoy some of the fête as well as helping out. She also gave a free drink to anyone who volunteered. It produced great 'social capital', because it wasn't an event *for* the local community but an event *by* the local community, since the free drink inspired most people to lend a hand. Not only did it make the whole event more manageable but it made it better too.

By paying attention at the planning stage and doing simple things like this, you can transform the fundraising experience. That is probably the greatest benefit of planning. The thing you want to leave people with is a memory bank full of happy and positive memories, because when you ask them again, the memories of the previous time are the first thing they will recall. To paraphrase Bob Dylan, you want people to remember it, not to never forget it. There is a world of difference between the two.

There is one more thing to add about planning. If you are doing the same thing you always did, then it will not click in the way that it once did because the outside context is changing all the time. It is like a machine where the cogs no longer fit smoothly but skip and jolt. The experience can quickly become a tiring and painful one, as you see people respond less generously and in fewer numbers year after year. By taking a step back and planning your fundraising, you give yourself time to acknowledge the changes within your own community and wider society, and to adapt your fundraising accordingly. That makes it fun again, and that is one of the biggest motivators for getting involved. By planning your fundraising, you can make sure you are looking after your fundraising not just for now, but for the future too.

The latent functions of work

Fundraising is not a solo activity if it is done well; so you will inevitably have to work well with others if you are to be a good fundraiser. Whether you are paid for your fundraising or you are a volunteer, at least some of your fundraising colleagues will also be volunteers. Volunteer management has whole textbooks written about it, so if you want to have a definitive in-depth view on managing volunteers, look away now. If not, read on.

There are an amazing number of disputes between paid and voluntary fundraisers. The latter often say that paying a fundraiser is effectively saying that voluntary fundraisers are no good, or that by paying a fundraiser the charity is wasting the money they raise, or not valuing what or, more often, who voluntary fundraisers are. Paid fundraisers and volunteer fundraisers can appear to be like oil and water, never mixing. There is often an assumption that, as organisations grow, it moves away from having a voluntary fundraising workforce to having a paid one. In one of my fundraising jobs, I had just started and was accosted by a volunteer fundraiser who prodded me in the chest and said 'You're not getting rid of me, sonny.'

This is one of the areas of fundraising I find most frustrating. There can be an elaborate game with some volunteer fundraisers where, as a paid fundraiser, you have to let everyone know that the volunteer fundraisers are better or more important than you are. However, you must not do this in an obvious way, because public statements about their brilliance would not fit in with their concept of 'selfless' volunteering. Hence, none of this can be explicitly stated but you both acknowledge it through asides, nudges and winks, both actual and metaphorical. You fit in around their diaries and not the other way round. At its worst, it can feel like there is almost a transaction going on: I will give my time to you in exchange for you acknowledging my greater contribution. A bit of a cynical take, perhaps, but the idea of volunteering being in some ways a transaction and volunteers getting something in return has merit. As a volunteer fundraiser myself, I can effortlessly swap sides, thinking I am not being thanked quite enough and those pesky paid staff are taking me for granted.

The reality is that, for many charities, both paid and voluntary fundraisers are necessary. There is something ironic about the division between the two, because the fundraising task is difficult enough as it is, and by being divided we have just made it even worse. It does not matter who manages volunteer fundraisers, whether they are paid or volunteers themselves, the volunteer fundraisers do need to be well managed. The wages of a volunteer are job satisfaction. That satisfaction is not easy to achieve, particularly in a business as difficult as fundraising, so if you are a manager of these volunteers you have your work cut out.

A sociologist called Jahoda identified that there are five 'latent' functions of work. These are the benefits of working, other than being paid. As such, they are a great template for creating satisfying jobs for volunteers. When you are putting together a task for a volunteer fundraiser, you need to think how you can give that task the following five attributes:

1. Structuring of time
2. Shared experience with non-family

3. Creativity, mastery and purpose
4. Status and identity
5. Activity, physical and mental effort

1. Structuring of time

Being in a paid job gives you a routine which is very helpful, even if it might not feel like it. It enables you to structure your day; it takes away some of the variables, and that is important because if you did not have those variables removed, you could be overwhelmed by the choices you face. If overwhelmed with choices, you may then decide to hide back under the duvet. You will not sit up moaning in bed 'Oh, I'm overwhelmed with choices', but you will *feel* overwhelmed and find you cannot even make the simplest decision like whether to have tea or coffee when you finally do get out of bed. Volunteers need a structuring of their day too; that is why it is important to agree when and where their volunteering will take place instead of a fluid 'I'll give you a call when we need you' arrangement. Agree the commitment in advance, how many hours a week, when they will be and when this commitment will be reviewed. It will show that you take their contribution seriously and enable them to structure their week around it.

2. Shared experience with non-family

It is important to have parts of our lives that are ours alone, not just lives shared with those with whom we live. It is something we can choose to talk about if we wish, but if we do not wish to, we can keep it to ourselves. It gives us a sense of control, a bit of mystery; it dissipates the intensity of family bonds and brings a variety into our relationships. These are all really important. Many people want to be able to tell their families over the washing-up about something interesting that has happened to them that day. Volunteering can provide this but needs to be structured to make sure it does. The volunteering role needs to involve mixing socially with others, ideally being part of a team, and time needs to be given for this. This needs to be quite a high percentage of the volunteering time, because full-time workers can have this shared experience spread over a whole week, whereas volunteers may need a week's worth within a few hours of volunteering.

3. Creativity, mastery and purpose

This sounds grand but it does not need to be. In one of my volunteer roles, I was really proud of the fact that I was the only one who knew how to change the colour toner on the photocopier. It is about knowing that you make an invaluable contribution to the process and, indeed, what that process achieves. Many volunteers are left in the dark (sometimes literally) as to why they are doing what they are doing and what difference (if any) it is making. They need to know in order to gain the psychological benefits from doing so. They also need to be able to improve the task they do by knowing how they can suggest improvements and how to ask for the resources they need.

4. Status and identity

'I'm only a volunteer' is the usual mantra. No one is 'only' anything, and it is important that the whole charity values what the volunteer does and that they are acknowledged for the part they play. The money volunteers can save is mind-boggling; much fundraising would be uneconomical without them. You could probably sum up volunteer management as making a volunteer feel valuable but not indispensable. Being indispensable can bring out the worst in people, but being valuable just brings out the best.

5. Activity, and physical and mental effort

When you are working with volunteers, make sure they are doing something! They cannot structure their work with you, as they often do not know what needs to be done; they need to be managed just like anyone else. Ensure that they do what they signed up to do and have the resources to do that task well. Their satisfaction comes from knowing they have done a job and not from having talked about doing it, so make sure that the talk turns into action or you will lose them.

This might all seem a bit much if all you want is volunteers to help at your Christmas fête. In reality, it can be very quick and easy to ensure you are delivering the five functions through your volunteering. It should be a quick mental checklist as you look at the work that you want people to do. Make sure that it has all five 'latent functions of work' and in all likelihood your volunteers will be happy to do it next time too.

OK, let's do the maths, shall we?

Part of the problem of fundraising is that fundraisers are so expensive. Correction. It is not fair to pick on fundraisers; they are often on the receiving end of terrible pay. It is probably fair to say that all paid staff are expensive. The advantage of other charity careers is that their jobs are not justified by one simple bottom line. Fundraisers are, or should be.

Charities (you may argue that this is unreasonable) actually expect paid fundraisers to raise more money than they cost. There are some circumstances where that probably is an unfair expectation. Fundraisers can sometimes stem the tide, so that the situation, while bad, is not as bad as it would have been if they had not been there. Suppose your charity brings in £1 million a year before the fundraiser starts, but then, when the fundraiser starts, so does the press exposé of your chief executive's expenses fraud; then for the £30,000-a-year fundraiser to bring in £30,000 is nothing short of miraculous. However, in the majority of cases, fundraisers should be raising funds, and more funds than it costs to employ them.

It is worth working out what that actually means. Say you earn £30,000 a year. You have to add on 20% to cover the additional costs of employing you in terms of employer's National Insurance and pension contributions and so on. Then add, say, £5,000 to cover the heat, light, telephone, internet usage, fixtures and fittings, and management time to support you (presuming you have a paid manager). Add in a further couple of grand for your travel expenses, another grand for marketing costs and another grand for 'miscellaneous' and you are costing £45,000 a year.

Take away your holiday entitlement and you are probably left with about 190 working days a year. In order to stand still you have 190 days in which to raise £45,000, except you do not have 190 days, of course. You need to take off 5 days for sickness each year, and at least 10 days for those mindless meetings that every organisation has, which you cannot avoid. Then add in a couple of days for 'mandatory training' and a few more for your fundraising conferences and you are down to 170 days.

Out of 365 days a year, fewer than half of them can be said to be productive work days. That means you need to raise over £260 every day just to pay back the costs of employing you. If you are more ambitious and you reckon you should raise £4 for every £1 spent, you need to be raising £1,000 a day. Every day.

So when you get roped in to help with an amateur dramatics 'charity production', which involves five days of costume-making, finding advertisers for the programme, selling tickets, obtaining a licence for the bar, getting some freebie sponsored lighting and setting out the chairs, the 'charity production' needs to raise over a grand to break even, and five grand to make an acceptable fundraising return.

So it's important to think through how you use your time, and ensure the fundraising ideas you are pursuing will give the return you need to make it worthwhile. Otherwise, you can end up costing your charity money rather than making it money. There, that has motivated you, hasn't it? Now get back to work.

And this too shall pass away

As an avid collector of quotes, there is a special place in my heart for Abraham Lincoln. There are hundreds and hundreds attributed to him, although I am not sure of the provenance of one I read on social media, namely 'Don't believe everything you read on the internet.' However, I am sure he would have said it if he had been born 200 years later.

Lincoln tells a great story where 'An Eastern monarch once charged his wise men to invent him a sentence to be ever in view, and which should be true and appropriate in all times and situations. They presented him the words: "And this, too, shall pass away."'

Lincoln delights in the way this phrase wards us off from the extremes of either complete euphoria or despair. If we are feeling euphoric, it tempers the euphoria, as we realise it will pass away. If we are feeling in despair, it tempers the despair, as we realise it too will pass away. For a man wrestling with the horrors of civil war, this aphorism clearly provided comfort. But it is equally true for us all.

One of the dangers of fundraising is to assume something that worked once will always work. This seems to be particularly true for charities that are very reluctant to let go of the fundraising methods that their founders used to create the charity in the first place ('To change is to honour the tradition' chapter on page 110 unpacks this more). There is, in part, a sentimental attachment to them, but there is also a temptation to think that something that created the cause in some way stands outside time – it must do to have brought this charity into being. That's nonsense, of course, but this isn't an entirely rational debate. So much of ourselves can be wrapped up in our fundraising it can be hard to separate out the two. But for even the best fundraising ideas, these too shall pass away.

So the reminder that 'this too shall pass away' is a helpful one. It's useful for us as fundraisers when something has gone well. Tempting as it is to think we have then cracked it, that from now on the fundraising will take care of itself, unfortunately these successes will also pass away. In reality, fundraising initiatives follow the same cycle as all projects: invention, planning, execution, monitoring and closure.

Rather than being dismayed by this reality, we should embrace it – everything has a shelf life, and we need to keep reinventing our fundraising and our practice to remain relevant and effective. Treasure good times when they happen, because they will not always be here. By acknowledging their fleeting nature, we can appreciate them more fully when they occur.

If the phrase is useful when things are going well, it comes into its own when they go badly. Hard as it may feel to imagine it at the time, the fundraising failures we all go through will pass and be replaced by fundraising successes – unless you are completely hopeless at fundraising, then you are probably beyond all hope, and if so, this book really won't help you. Stoically endure bad times, for they too will not always be here, and there is a comfort in realising, if nothing else, that they will eventually pass.

Matthew Syed, once an international sportsperson and now a journalist and author, has written compellingly about the gold-medal-winning Japanese ice skater Shizuka Arakawa. She was the 2004 world champion and the 2006

Olympic champion, becoming the first Japanese skater to win an Olympic gold medal in figure skating. By any measure, she has had an extraordinarily successful career. And yet, she estimates that she has fallen over more than 20,000 times in her training. Over 20,000 times she failed to do what she wanted to, namely stay upright, and it is her willingness to keep going through these failures that enabled her to succeed. Whether she muttered to herself 'and this, too, shall pass away' as she hit the rink floor yet again, I can't say, but she certainly lived by this mantra.

We often see failure as a disaster to be avoided, but we would be much better to acknowledge its inevitability and learn from it. Failure can also be our finest hour if we react to it well, and it is how we react to failure rather than the avoiding of failure that dictates how our organisations prosper and grow. Failure, like success, is momentary and a secret to our own well-being is to remember this. 'And this, too, shall pass away' – a sentiment for all times.

My bubble, you squeak

'He was the perfect kind of neighbour; he kept himself to himself.' This was a quote from a next-door neighbour of a newly discovered serial murderer I recall reading in a news story some years ago. Our 'perfect' relationships are the ones where we engage with the people concerned as little as possible.

It is unarguable that our society is becoming ever more individualised. Go back a few centuries and you would be lucky to see a few hundred people during your whole lifetime. Now, we see hundreds of people a day. The no-doubt-at-times-claustrophobic village life has largely disappeared. In those days, everyone knew everyone else's business. This was also a necessity: people needed to stick together to be safe. You had to be in with the 'in' crowd or you were dead with the 'out' crowd. It was quite simple.

As human beings we were used to finding our niche within a fairly defined and stable community. Fast forward a few centuries and it is no surprise that we are bewildered. We see millions of people within our lifetimes, the majority of whom we will never speak to. We do business every day with people we do not know. The threat of exclusion was a marvellous disciplinary mechanism; it made people behave and do what they said they would do. Nowadays, we have laws instead, which is a far less efficient and a much more unwieldy way of achieving the same thing. The irony, of course, is that our need for trust, love, acceptance, kindness and so on is just the same but it is now so much harder to achieve because we do not know with whom we are dealing. We are hardwired to look for and need these things, but we are much more vulnerable to being exploited because of that need. Looked at in this way, our lives are more pitiable than those of our ancestors. I had a good friend who was an inorganic chemist and would snort at such sentimentality. 'I'm sure chewing on a stick does something for toothache, but I'd prefer a local anaesthetic' or words to that effect. I am not trying to dismiss the wonderful march of science and technology, but look at its consequences for us as human beings.

We are still preoccupied with relationships with other human beings, however advanced our society is in so many ways. We still want strong, deep and committed relationships. However, a consequence of global communications, cheaper travel and all of that is that we have brought a mobility and transience to our communities, which compromise the relationships we seek. Because the trust is not there, because we do not know who we are dealing with half the time, we are increasingly withdrawing into our 'bubbles', building largely self-contained lives for our own protection.

This impacts on fundraising, because giving to charities, especially grass-roots local community ones, is absolutely dependent upon not seeing ourselves as being removed. It requires an implicit understanding and agreement that we are all inter-connected and that we have a responsibility for each other. We do not ask people to give money because they have exhausted every other way of spending on themselves. We ask them to sacrifice something that they would have enjoyed or liked in order that someone else might have something that they need.

If there is not an understanding that this is something we should do, our work as fundraisers becomes immeasurably harder. We not only have to win the argument that *our* cause deserves their support; we have first of all to win the argument that *any* cause deserves their support. If we do not engage with this reality, we will be like lumbering dinosaurs fighting over the reducing vegetation, without any of us thinking about why the vegetation is disappearing in the first place. If there is no more vegetation, it does not matter whether you win your fight with your enemy dinosaur or not; you will both end up dead. Part of the role of a fundraiser is to plant generosity within a funder, to show them the worth in being generous and indeed how necessary it is for them to cultivate it. Our problem is that we are not judged on such heady and worthy principles; the 'bottom line' analysis does not measure such things, but if we do not do this, then who will?

How do we get people to pop their particular bubbles? I think personally there is merit in starting from the basis that most people are, to be honest, pretty frightened by many things. We need to structure opportunities for people to engage with others in as non-threatening a way as possible. I used to work for a charity that, I would argue, got some things wrong (such as employing me, to be honest). It did, though, in one part of its existence, do something absolutely wonderfully right. It would encourage people to spend a weekend in London, having a smashing day on the Saturday with shopping, visits to museums and galleries and a show in the evening. After the show, they would go to one of the charity's homeless hostels or do a soup run. The next day they would meet staff who worked in a women's refuge, or some who worked at the charity's drugs clinics. You get the picture. It was the juxtaposition between the good things in life (that the supporter had) and the hard things that others experienced. The crucial thing was seeing it face to face, realising that those who were supported by the charity were actually the same as them. Through bad luck, twists of fate, poor decisions, social injustice or whatever, their lives had taken divergent paths. Intrinsically, however, they were the same.

Your cause may not be so dramatic, but it will still be about people. Look at the way you do your fundraising and the way you communicate with your supporters. In what ways do you reinforce the relationship between them and your charity's beneficiaries? When your supporters hear you talk about your cause, are they thinking how similar they are to the beneficiaries or do they think they are a different species entirely? Granted, it is probably the latter if you fundraise for an animal charity, but I would still argue the point, even in that scenario. It is vital to show the connections, not the separateness or differences, between the benefactor and the beneficiary. It improves the quality of the donation and changes the donor at the same time.

Realpolitik

Realpolitik is politics that are based on practicality, or urgency. It is pragmatism in political form. It does not rely on moral, ideological or ethical principles but on what works to achieve a goal. It is gloriously and unashamedly functional.

There is, I would argue, an important place for realpolitik in all charities, but the exclusive pursuit of it can be catastrophic. If you could be even vaguely described as ideological, you are probably going to find some of this chapter hard work. Many people are attracted to charities because they are perceived as counter-culture. While arguably our Western world becomes ever more materialistic, consumption-driven, competitive, egocentric and selfish, the charity world offers a beacon to a more just and equitable land. Charities are about compassion, the deep rather than the ephemeral, justice, hope, a new heaven and a new earth.

That is, perhaps, with the exception of fundraising, because fundraising is not socialism; it can be more like rampant and untamed capitalism.

As a very good friend, who happens to be an exemplary man of the cloth, put it, 'money buggers up everything'. Money, though, is what fundraising is all about. It brings the filthy lucre right into the heart of the pristine, nay saintly, heart of a charity. The whole ambiguity about money and wealth is exposed by fundraising. It is a big responsibility to bear.

I once had an amusing conversation with a grants officer for a very large grant-making trust. We both agreed that it would be far more equitable to have a quality threshold which, if passed, guaranteed funding. It would also, regrettably, guarantee the bankruptcy of the grant-making trust concerned.

As there isn't as much funding as everyone needs, inevitably charities compete for funding, which leads inexorably to the survival of the fundraising fittest. Economics is, so they taught me at O-Level, all about the allocation of scarce resources, and so is fundraising. There is not enough to go round, so that inescapably means that some will win and some will lose.

If you are in competition, you do not need to be perfect; you just need to be a little bit better than your competitor. Who is most likely to give to your cause? Well, fairly obviously, to my mind, it is someone who has given to a similar cause before. They are far more likely to give than someone who has never given before. Consequently, if you follow this train of thought, to be the most cost-effective at your fundraising you need to appeal to the donors of other charities and just be that little bit better than they are when it comes to service delivery and fundraising. This is the exact opposite of 'changing-the-world' fundraising. This is, if anything, 'regressing-the-world' fundraising. Taken to an extreme, you could then be trying to squash the competition so that there are fewer charities out there battling with you for the money that is up for grabs.

How does this make you feel? It makes me feel very uneasy, but there is a logic to it, however unappealing. Getting people to give to your cause is hard enough as it is; getting them to agree to the idea of giving in the first place just makes the whole thing immeasurably harder. You simply have to go for those most likely to give, and if that means another charity loses those supporters, well, maybe that's just the way things are.

This is the confusing and paradoxical moral world that fundraising inhabits. Pure realpolitik can take us down a path which might not be somewhere we would want to go. We need to take a step back and work out what we are comfortable with and what we are not. It can't all be pragmatism, in other words.

For example, I worked for a charity which needed to increase its legacy income and, as ever, wanted to spend as little as possible on fundraising. I therefore explained to the trustees that those most likely to leave legacies to charities were single, elderly, poor females. This meant that if we were to raise the most money for the least cost, we needed to do some demographic analysis of postcodes, find the areas with the highest incidence of such people and focus our legacy fundraising in those areas. Without exception, the trustees were appalled. This was absolutely not what they identified charities as being for. In other words, they, and indeed the charity, had a moral compass, and things were not as straightforward as saying raise as much money as you can for as little cost as possible. Ethics and morals are important too. Realpolitik has its limits.

While on the subject of politics, it is worth reflecting on the changing political climate in all these debates. By and large, in the past, many charities believed they existed because they were doing something important that the state had missed. The logic of this argument then leads you towards the conclusion that charities like this would aspire to their work being taken on by the state when they have proved its need. The charity then skips off to find another unmet need or it folds up as its work has been done.

However, this way of looking at things now feels a bit quaint. The direction of travel is now going in totally the opposite direction. There is a growing understanding that charities can actually do what the state does, but do it better.

On the other hand, if all the charity does is deliver public sector work, where the need is defined by government, the means of meeting that need are defined by government and the funding is given by government, then that to me means that the charity is the government in all but name. If it walks like a duck and quacks like a duck, it must be a duck. I know that is not exactly a popular point of view, but one of my deep frustrations with charities occurs when they become obsessed with survival above all else. They scrabble around getting a whole load of disconnected grants, which certainly provides lots of activity but gives no obvious answer as to why they should be doing it. At some point, you have to ask whether the accumulation of contracts for public sector services can really be classed as a charitable activity in itself. To my mind, and I know this is old-fashioned but I do not care, charities are here to do themselves out of a job. They should ask whether they are pursuing grants to keep the organisation going as an end in itself, or whether it is genuinely in order to continue to meet the needs of their beneficiaries.

Some 180 years ago, the school I used to work for defined the need (educating deaf children), met that need (ran a school) and funded the need (fundraising). In the more recent past, the government (both local and central) had started defining the need, deciding on how the need is met and deciding how much it will cost. Bluntly, the charity had gone from setting its own agenda to responding to someone else's. To me, that is not what charities are about, and one of my challenges was to bring in new income streams so that the charity could get back to setting its own agenda. This is important for fundraising, because any organisation needs to know where it is heading. If it genuinely believes that it is not only better than the public sector at identifying need but also at meeting that need, I would argue that fundraising should always be an important part of the overall income for the charity if it is to avoid 'mission drift'.

Ergo, what are the ambitions for your charity? If fundraising is always going to be a valuable part of funding – because it allows you to set the agenda – then you need to think about fundraising not as a passing fad but as a permanent part of the furniture (but one that will need re-covering fairly often). You also need to think about realpolitik and its limitations for a charity like yours.

Emotional intelligence

It was a Eureka moment for me. I was discussing the travails of management with someone far better at it than me. He explained a theory that he found very helpful when having to deal with the nincompoops that he was supposed to manage. It is a very simple theory, but I have found it invaluable ever since. Namely, that it is easier to change knowledge than behaviour. If I had known this when I started my management 'career', I could have saved myself many a disastrous appointment.

So often when we look to recruit people, and this can include recruiting volunteers to organise a community barbecue, we judge most highly people's technical skill (how quickly they can light the barbecue), while ignoring the fact that they might be so overbearing and irritating while doing it that no one will actually want to come to the barbecue. This happens all the time. It is a knee-jerk reaction for many and can cause much wasted time and energy. Frankly, the last thing your fundraising needs is someone who sends everyone running for the hills as soon as they hone into view. People are often kind and generous, but it can stretch that kindness and generosity to breaking point if they have to spend the entire event with someone they find profoundly irritating.

The reality is that most of the things that fundraisers do are not actually that difficult, nor do they take years of practice. You can pick up the skills relatively quickly as long as you are a good listener. Your technical knowledge should not be important. I take an inordinate amount of pride in acquiring a working knowledge of many different things, knowing just enough to appear to the media as someone authoritative. Moving from a hospice to a school for the deaf – 'death' to 'deaf', as someone described it to me – I set myself a challenge to learn enough about this totally new subject to be able to write a plausible article for a magazine. I did it in six months. I am not that brainy, so really anyone should be able to do this.

Accordingly, if knowledge is not the thing, what is? It helps to be numerate, literate and to know how to turn on a PC. Beyond that, what are you left with? I would argue that the really big thing you need is emotional intelligence. Ivory towers across the globe don't always agree whether it should be called emotional intelligence or emotional knowledge, but we will not go into that. The important thing to realise is that the ability to understand yourself and others is probably the most important gift a fundraiser can have. It is not just because it means you can get on with your fellow fundraisers, but also because you will be much better at relating to your supporters.

It is difficult to describe an example without sounding big-headed, so let's say that there was a fundraiser called Jonty de Bernhardt Woof who was talking to someone who had recently been bereaved, and who said she wanted to organise a fundraising event for the charity he worked for because of the care it had given her close friend. The thing is that, while that was what she said, what she meant was 'I want to tell you how much I miss my friend, and I want to cry and cry.' The fundraising was just a mechanism, and if Jonty hadn't realised this, he would have been both a useless fundraiser and no help to someone in obvious distress.

Fundraising is about empathy, connections, emotions, relationships and compassion; it is not about mechanisms, making things, structures, 'boxes' and all the other things that arguably the left side of the brain loves.

Emotional intelligence has four basic aspects: self-awareness, self-management, social awareness and relationship management. It's worth unpacking the first two particularly for fundraising. Self-awareness is really important. Many charities deal in fairly distressing situations. As a fundraiser, you need to realise when you are being affected negatively by the business you are in. You also need to realise when you are in danger of getting people to do what you want, rather than what they want. Self-management is crucial too, particularly in something as woolly as fundraising. How good are you at putting a limit to your fundraising? What do you do to relax? How do you switch off? How do you cope with the inherent powerlessness in fundraising? How do you cope with the rejection that makes up 90% of your job? How do you cope with the fact that most of the people you meet will not understand what you do or why?

The powerlessness is worth dwelling on. Ultimately, you cannot make people give to your cause. It is a tough one to accept, but it is true. Your job satisfaction is reliant on their generosity. It is so easy to try to short-cut this dependence by manipulating people into doing what you want, but, if it works at all, it is only a short-term fix that will also break the relationship. The concept of being in control is very important to many people, and consequently to be comfortable with not being in control is atypical. I would argue that the concept of being in control is absurd, false, misleading and ultimately harmful, and therefore to be released from it – by fundraising showing you that it is all of these things – is a blessing. Not everyone will see it like this. Whether you agree with this way of thinking or not, it is important that you can be happy in a powerless situation. Otherwise, the stress will kill you. You will either get into a vicious cycle of alienating more and more people by badgering them into giving money and thus making the pool of potential givers smaller and smaller, or you will try to claim control over something which you actually know you have no control whatsoever over. Neither of these options is particularly attractive.

Planning your way out of a bag

Often charities are not very good at being self-critical. We feel uneasy about being critical of work when, due to its very nature, the people concerned cannot separate themselves from the people-centred nature of their work. For that reason, to criticise their work is to criticise them. As a result, charities can sometimes be the last organisations to confront bad practice, which is ironic really because, bearing in mind how important our work is, we should be the first to do so.

One of the frustrations of being a fundraiser is that people will watch you like a hawk, while being a blind chicken where their own work is concerned. Here is a true example. I worked for a charity that was creating a truly innovative project. It was a telephone counselling service. It would run on a Sunday, because that was apparently often the most difficult day of the week for the client group. Trained volunteers would run this dedicated telephone line. The media absolutely loved this story. It had everything: a bit of suffering, a noble and worthy charity, people giving their time to help others. The publicity for it was amazing; all the media we approached ran the story. The launch day dawned, and during that day the charity received two calls all day. The following Sunday there were no calls. The Sunday after that, there were again no calls. Then the project was pulled.

The thing is that the people who came up with this project were really great people, excellent professionals, utterly dedicated and inspiring. However, the lack of project management skills meant that they were seriously ill-equipped to set up a new project like this. Yet setting up projects is exactly what fundraisers are about, because we do it all the time. Have a look at this:

Project phase	Fundraising project	Charity service
Research	focus group of supporters	focus group of users
Creation	inflatable sumo-wrestling competition	advice line for those in debt
Development	assess risks	assess risks
	create budget	create budget
	research suppliers	increase phone lines
	identify costs	train volunteers
	test with market audience	test with market audience
	create timetable	create launch timetable
Refinement	finalise project	finalise project
Communication	start advertising	start advertising
Delivery	launch event	launch event
Monitor	check event logistics	record percentage of calls and review
	check pledges to money raised	
Evaluation	complete post-event 'wash up' (i.e. an evaluation meeting)	full review after three months

As you can see, the processes for planning a sumo-wrestling event are the same as for starting a debt advice line or establishing a drop-in centre for bereaved people, or a pets' hospital, or an after-school club, or a soup run and so on. You get the picture. For many people who work for charities, the establishment of a new piece of work is a relatively rare phenomenon. It is normally the same old same old, and a good thing too. People's needs do not change that quickly, nor do the best means of meeting them, and too much change can be disorientating. There are some times, though, when practice should be changed or a new project should begin. In these cases, surely it makes sense to use the skills and experience of those who establish projects on a daily basis?

The reasons that fundraisers' project planning experience is rarely used are various and complex. Sometimes fundraisers do not have the confidence to do it. Other times they do not actually realise that they are experts in project development and management; they do not reflect enough to realise this. Sometimes other charity staff merely tolerate fundraisers and want as little to do with them as possible. Whatever the reason, by keeping fundraisers away from the charity's core activity, the ones who lose out are the ones that the charity is supposed to be helping.

When I became Chief Executive of a charity that runs a special needs school, there was a fair bit of tutting and sighing within the special needs field. How on earth could someone who wasn't a teacher – was in *marketing*, for heaven's sake – possibly lead an educational charity and, more specifically, a school? Being a Yorkshireman, I have always been quite blunt and my reply was 'By being a better business, we will be a better school.' It does not fit with what some imagine a school to be, but as the days passed, I grew more convinced that it is true. By researching what the needs are, working out how most effectively to meet those needs, recruiting and training the right staff, making sure the service provision is all affordable, ensuring people know about what we do, ensuring we deliver what we said we would, and checking our effectiveness and periodically reviewing things, I am instilling key disciplines that all successful organisations need. The same can be true throughout just about every charity, providing the charity will let fundraisers loose with their project management skills. In view of the fact that this will make a charity's work better, it is a scandal that it does not happen all the time.

To change is to honour the tradition

The British really seem to have something about honouring tradition. In what other country could the National Trust evoke such impassioned debate? We wish to preserve a former way of life so that we can observe it, record it and learn about it. It was not always like this. In times gone by, if there was a major fire in a palace, the royalty in question would jump for joy because it gave them a chance to get rid of the hideous old stuff and put in something new, modern and chic. When part of Windsor Castle burnt down, we took almost unnatural delight in returning it to exactly the way it was. Of course, it is no longer the original, it just looks like it, but that is enough. We would prefer to put in a replica of something that was old rather than put in something original, authentic and modern (there goes my knighthood).

Exactly the same kind of mindset is found in many charities. Many of them could have the slogan 'a rolling stone gathers no moss, but we quite like moss, actually'. The instinct is to be cautious, tentative even. The irony is that charities are almost designed to be free of any kind of conservative thinking. We are not part of some monolithic national public service, weighed down by systems, processes and bureaucracy. We are small, light, nimble and able to change direction relatively easily if the need arises.

However, I would argue that in most major areas of charity activities we tend to be too cautious. This can often go unnoticed because, I suspect, people have had a rather unquestioning attitude to charities. This is because if they are seen to be critical, it could be considered very 'bad form'. Many people also think charities are run only by volunteers, and so it would seem mean to set the same standards for them as for paid staff. For whatever reason, charities have historically tended to get a fairly easy ride, although this is clearly changing. As a result, the limitations of conservative thinking are often hidden from public view in many areas of a charity's life.

I am not sure why some charities are so conservative, but I think part of the reason is a version of the founder's syndrome. Here, the very drive and determination that someone has in order to form a charity are the very things that bring it to the brink of closure, because the drive and determination morph into intransigence and a failure to delegate. It is something to do with the investment or over-investment people can have in charities, where people identify with a cause to such an extent that they become indivisible from it. Thus, if a charity changes what it does, it is somehow insulting those who did whatever they did previously. People's identities become dependent on things staying exactly the same.

From my experience, this happens a huge amount with charity fundraising. We have to keep doing some form of fundraising, even though it does not really cut it anymore, because otherwise Mr or Mrs Malarkey will kick up merry hell and the grief they would cause would be worse than the hassle of organising a futile fundraising venture. It is all really odd. There is probably a PhD in it somewhere: 'The transference of self and identity from person to fundraising venture in charities in Bedfordshire between 2000 and 2020'.

While the organisers of these appeals and events may not wane in their enthusiasm, the same cannot be said of everyone else. If people do not like a fundraising event or idea, then by and large they will ignore it. They may support something for a while, out of guilt, normally, or loyalty to the organiser, but the decline is inevitable and continual.

If you think of the work your cause does, it is probable that people will be reasonably reassured to know that it is largely doing what it has always done; for example, 'we continue to research the causes of cancer'. With fundraising, I suspect, the same is not always true; 'we are still mainly fundraising through our annual summer fête' will not so much reassure people as bore them. There is often an unspoken expectation from givers that fundraising is changing, adapting and growing. It is expected to change with the times, to see new trends and to react to the ways people live their lives now. A great example of this is the rise in online or contactless giving. It reflects the fact that people use cash far less than they used to, but also that, certainly within churches, people give significantly more when giving in these ways compared to cash. The very nature of the giving mechanism encourages greater generosity.

The best example of the 'trapped-in-history' fundraising method must be street collections. What are we doing? What message is it sending? 'We can survive on a few coppers from a handful of people' probably. When I ask 'normal' (that is, non-fundraising) people about fundraising, they always, always, always first talk about street collections. And how much money do we raise through street collections nationally? A tiny percentage of all income raised, I reckon. People perceive fundraising to be about frozen people wearing garish sashes 'not shaking' a tin in a shopping centre near them. Is it any surprise that fundraising has a bad image? I am genuinely impressed at the brave and hardy souls who actually raise money in this way, but I cannot believe that their time could not be better spent.

There is a wonderful irony in the fact that so many charities are hidebound by a love of tradition. These charities only came about because they previously had a modern and contemporary outlook. They were identifying an unmet need and raising funds in the best way possible, which is the way that most people liked. People did not always love raffles, golf days or summer fêtes, but they did when a large number of charities were formed. Hence that is how the fundraising started. If we are to be true to our founders, we should copy their mindset, not their practice. We should, just as they did, look at what would be the most effective way of giving *now*. When you are founding a charity, it is an exciting but desperate time. You have not got the time to humour people by doing things that do not actually work very well. You just do whatever works best.

Charities are not some peripheral 'spare some change if you've got any and you've got the time and you want a sticker, but don't worry if you don't' organisations. They are vital, essential and central to the whole way our society operates. Fundraising cannot be seen as some retro kind of throwback to a bygone era; our practice should be thunderingly and obviously contemporary. So if we really want to follow in the footsteps of those who have gone before, we should do whatever works best now. To be radical now is to honour the tradition.

Poor people can't afford cheap goods

One of the classic fundraising mistakes is to confuse something that is cheap with something that is good value. So much of a charity's resources are bought on the cheap, in a sale or on 'special offer', that it is hardly surprising if we struggle to be competent. Faced with either five sound purchases or ten cheap ones, we normally go for the latter, because we like the idea of achieving as much as we can. Unfortunately, we end up doing ten things badly rather than five things well, and as a result we end up doing less.

Many years ago, I knew of a very well-known charity that bought a cheap database they then used to store tens of thousands of entries on it. It decided to mail occasional givers asking them to become regular givers. Unfortunately, the database was total rubbish and so it could not sort properly. This meant that the regular givers received a request to become regular givers. The end result of buying this particular cheap item was money wasted on an appeal and the most important group of donors feeling their donations were neither noticed nor valued.

One of my childhood memories is of going with my grandparents to Dewsbury market where we would listen to the market stall-holders shouting out their wares (that is probably illegal now, noise pollution or something, but it was great fun then). I loved the drama of it, how they worked the crowd. My Grandma was savvy, though. She enjoyed the spectacle as much as I did, but she only bought what she wanted and not what seemed to be a bargain. This is what we should aspire to: do not hand money over just for the sake of it but do not compromise on the quality of what you need either.

Part of the reluctance to invest properly is the belief that all charities should have the aroma of a burning martyr. No one should look as if they receive adequate resources to do their work. Everything should be cheap and broken. Doing charity work should be fighting overwhelming odds with no resources, in a desperate and futile attempt to change unchangeable behaviours, people and societies. The idea that charities should be successful, and that they need to invest in order to be so, is still a notion that jars with many. Charities are still populated by humans, not saints. Other organisations know that if you treat your staff well and give them the tools they need, they will be more successful. I have been with too many charities where I had to work in hideous 1960s south-facing offices with absolutely no ventilation, never mind air conditioning. The office temperature would be in the mid 30s regularly, and still you were expected to function normally. No other organisation would accept this, and you are supposed to be doing more important work than a 'normal' business, so why do charities persist with it?

Poor people cannot afford cheap goods because they cannot afford to replace things that break quickly or never do what they were supposed to do. Similarly, charities cannot afford to replace dodgy office furniture, IT equipment or telephones, and so we must ensure that we do not buy cheaply the first time round. A healthy organisation is one that invests sensibly but substantially in its operations. You know an organisation is in trouble when you see it stop spending money on its infrastructure. It is looking for a quick saving, but by doing so it is harming its long-term prospects.

This is often particularly true in fundraising. It is the sister of marketing, and marketing is often the first to get the chop in a for-profit business when times are hard. That makes no sense, and what makes equally little sense is chopping a fundraising budget in a charity when it hits hard times. I am told by people who know more about this than I do that there is no correlation between an organisation's current marketing spend and its effectiveness. However, apparently, there is a correlation between an organisation's marketing spend three years previously and its current effectiveness. In the same way that marketing activity takes time to permeate through a for-profit organisation, fundraising takes time to permeate through a not-for-profit organisation. Good, sensible, patient investment is crucial for successful fundraising.

If your fundraising budget is very close to zero, you may be struggling to map your own experience against this chapter. What you need to do is take a step back and look at what you are expected to do. You will probably find that one of the 'cheap goods' in question is you! You are probably being asked to do far too much in far too short a time and with far too little support. From my experience, the normal 'investment failure' in charities is with its people, not its equipment, materials or land. So, list what you are expected to do and then objectively critique the resource you are given against what you actually need. What will normally happen is that you can still do things within your miniscule budget, but not as much as you have been doing 'on the cheap'. Therefore, draw back your level of activity to the point where you know you can resource that activity well. Then, once you have it under control, you can start to increase your activity as the greater investment becomes available.

In his autobiography, Roald Dahl tells the story of when he was a pilot in the Second World War. He was supposed to be providing air cover for the British armed forces in Greece against the advancing German army and air force. Nearly half the German air force was engaged in taking Greece. Roald Dahl had only six other pilots with him to protect the British army that was in retreat. It was totally futile, tragic and deeply depressing. We are lucky that a lack of investment in our fundraising does not reap the consequences it did for them. The lack of investment, though, is still futile and depressing, whatever the context. It is an uncomfortable message, but all organisations need to be told when they are asking for too much from too little. If you do not deliver this message, the organisation will think it is your failing, not its own, that leads to the inevitable fundraising failure.

Svengali fundraising

If there is one thing I sincerely hope never to hear again, it is a trustee of a charity telling me they think fundraisers should be paid commission. It is normally perceived as a clever way of making sure that you do not pay fundraisers to not raise money. It is an understandable concern; there have been some fundraisers who have left a charity in a worse financial state than it was in when they first started because they have not raised even half of their salary. However, this perception is utterly simplistic and potentially very dangerous.

Let me tell you a true story. A charity paid a fundraiser a basic (very poor) salary and then said he could have 10% of any new money raised. The charity did not define what 'new money' was, but it would seem reasonable to assume that this was money that had not been pledged before the fundraiser had arrived and was from supporters who had not previously given or given in that way or at that level. This charity was in the fortunate position of being very popular with the public and, as a result, the fundraiser spent a good proportion of his time operating as a fund-facilitator rather than a fundraiser. In other words, many people wanted to give, and his job was to enable them to do so. Fund-facilitating is still very important, of course, and many charities do not think about the importance of this as much as they should, but it is probably not what the charity had in mind when it came up with its cunning contract. So far, so bad. The fundraiser is effectively being given 10% of income which he may or may not have had any involvement in, and it may not have been a decisive influence anyway. It gets worse, much worse. A lovely old lady wrote to the charity asking for information about it. The fundraiser diligently responded, and a little file of correspondence built up between the two. Time passes and someone opens the post to find the charity is to be a beneficiary of this lady's will and will receive a gift worth several million pounds. Now this was new money, which the fundraiser clearly had some involvement in raising, so all of a sudden the clever wheeze of 10% commission on new donations doesn't look so clever after all.

By looking at what will happen if the fundraiser is successful, you can often get a good picture of whether your idea for the way of paying them is a good one. There are numerous problems with how commission fundraising is perceived and here are a few. First, what would the public think if they found that 10% of each donation is not going to the charity but directly to the fundraiser's pocket? Second, commission fundraising can attract those who are looking for a quick buck and do not care about the consequences for the charity's reputation. Third, it does not acknowledge the fact that some funds are facilitated rather than raised, and there is a big difference in skill and effort between the two. Finally, if the fundraiser is really successful, it becomes absurd, with fundraisers receiving hundreds of thousands of pounds for relatively little work. You may say that that is fine because they bring in money that otherwise the charity would not have. I would argue that that is far too short-term an attitude, and that if you do not fundraise in ways that your supporters accept, they will soon find causes that do.

Therefore, should fundraisers be judged on results, even if they are not paid according to them? In a nutshell, my response would be, 'yes, kind of'. That is to say, fundraisers are in the business of raising funds, which is why they exist, and if they are not judged in this way, it would be comparable to a milkman or woman being paid whether they deliver milk or not.

Nonetheless, it is not quite that simple. I would argue that fundraisers do not have some Svengali-like power over supporters that makes them hand over cash irrespective of whether they want to. Good fundraising is only one part of successfully raising funds. You have to make sure that the core business of the charity is good and that the work you are raising money for is sound and proven to be needed. The charity must be well governed and managed, efficient and economical. If your plans for a village hall expect its costing to be £3 million and you are putting in bids for funding that are up against other village hall projects that cost less than half of that, then you will probably not do very well, however good you are.

For that reason, when analysing whether you are being an effective fundraiser, you (and/or your charity) need to look at your work within the context of the organisation as a whole. You also need to think about timescales. Fundraising is basically a relationship business, and relationships take time to build. Good fundraisers look for in-depth and committed relationships with their funders, which by their very nature do not lead to instant, high-impact responses. Remember that people give for many good reasons, but also for many bad ones. People may give money just to make you go away. The results may look good to start with, but that will soon fade as people change phone numbers, jobs, addresses and even identities in order to avoid you.

I do not believe that fundraisers can make people give, and I do not believe fundraising effectiveness is immune from the quality or lack of it within the rest of the charity. I am also wary of immediate-impact fundraisers. To me, to judge a fundraiser fairly you need to see how well they really understand and care about the cause, really understand the charity's supporters and really understand their role in raising money. If they have these three understandings, they will probably come good, however long it takes. Finally, do remember, as Snoopy used to say, that nobody's perfect, and who wants to be a nobody?

Overcoming your fundraising phobia

In this book, the various chapters delve into the intricacies and complexities of the noble art and science that is fundraising. As you can tell, I have no problem with wrestling with fundraising complexities, being fascinated by it and practising it to various degrees of success for over 30 years. But, sometimes, even a fundraising zealot like myself will acknowledge that not everyone is similarly enamoured nor, frankly, has the time for a deep dive into the fundraising seas.

I was once asked what I would say to someone who was not only unenamoured with fundraising but positively hostile to it, verging on allergic, but had to do it anyway. For example, someone wants to volunteer in a development charity project over the summer but needs to raise £10,000 to do that. They are hugely motivated by the volunteering but utterly terrified of the fundraising needed for it. And that's fair enough, the talents and drivers for one are not the same as for the other, so there's no reason they should be thrilled about both. If you are faced with a sizeable fundraising challenge which is inescapable, what is the simplest and most focused way of using your time to enable the fundraising to be done? And so the 12-step plan to overcome your fundraising phobia was born.

Before skipping through these 12 stages like a spring lamb, it's important to acknowledge that 12 stages is a lot if you are fundraising phobic. However, better to be upfront, I think, and I genuinely believe you need all these 12 stages for your fundraising to be successful. Besides, some are not particularly time consuming, but they do still all need to be done.

Last point before diving in – these stages assume you are taking on your fundraising challenge as a team, not an individual, because that's the best way to do it by far – for your fundraising effectiveness, and indeed for your own sanity. The team can be a team of two if needs be, but try and avoid solitary fundraising if you can.

1. Identify need

To paraphrase Julie Andrews, we should start at the beginning, which is a very good place to start. What is the need you are trying to meet? Now turn it around, what will change when that need is met? How much will it cost? How long will it take? That's the basis of your fundraising ask.

2. Internal audit

Not the most grippingly titled of stages but important nonetheless. You need to look at what fundraising treasure you have hidden within the group of people who will be fundraising. What talents, experience, contacts and resources do you have? What can you all give towards your fundraising target (people will often only donate as much as the person asking them has given)?

3. Research sources

Having done an internal audit, look outside to see what potential there is out there. Identify all potential funding sources, however remote a possibility you think they might be at this stage.

4. Agree ethics
Might seem a bit of an overkill if all you want to do is raise £10,000 for playground equipment, but you'd be surprised. It is miles better to have this conversation now rather than in the midst of a fundraising campaign when one of the team has spent an age warming up a company or individual that the rest of the team feel is completely inappropriate.

5. Cost/benefit analysis
Work through the different funding sources and agree which are most likely to raise the most for the least cost (in time, money and energy). This activity stops you wasting that time, money and energy on things which sound great but cost more to carry out than you raise. You can save yourself a lot of heartache and frustration if you do this stage well.

6. Establish team roles
You know what you want to raise funds for, and the difference it will make, and you know what skills and contacts you have between you and what the potential source of funds are. Now you need to establish the team roles, so everyone is clear on what they are contributing and who will do what. This is key, because you'll then be accountable to each other for delivering on your specific role and tasks.

7. Craft your fundraising pitch
Pull together what you have discovered so far in the previous stages to agree the fundraising message. It is often helpful

to use the discipline of the 'elevator pitch' (it's American, as you can probably guess). Namely, you have the time it takes to travel from one floor to the next in a lift to communicate your fundraising pitch. This exercise makes you cut out the unnecessary flummery and succinctly communicate the key points.

8. Plan it

Pull together a plan which summarises what you will do. This does not need to be long or complex; indeed, it is better if it is neither. Just list the tasks to be done, the expected outcome, who leads on it, who else needs to support it, what resources you need and when it will happen. Use this plan to keep track of the different activities you will be doing and to keep you all focused.

9. Warm up funders

Start conversations with potential funders early, before your fundraising campaign is formally launched. Funders always like being involved early, and the initial feedback can help shape the fundraising as it is rolled out.

10. Launch

I know, you've done nine steps before actually asking people for money. For fundraising, preparation is everything, or at least 75%. To be clear, a 'launch' can be as simple as meeting down the pub to say the fundraising campaign is now in its public phase, it doesn't need to be hugely elaborate. Important, though, that the campaign itself is launched with a clear end date, as it needs to be time limited to have impetus and focus (see 'Thanks a million' on page 39 for more on this).

11. Deliver

Make those fundraising asks, roll out the social media activities and engage with media organisations. Keep in touch with each other as you do so, checking back on the plan to make sure you are not being distracted during this crucial delivery phase. Track the money as it comes in, thank everyone and celebrate with all your donors when the target is reached.

12. Evaluate

Don't miss the opportunity to reflect on what you have achieved and what you have learned. This might not be the only fundraising activity you are ever involved with, so take the chance to distil your learning so you can use it next time.

There are no guarantees in fundraising, but our job as fundraisers is to increase the odds of success, and following these 12 stages definitely does that. For those who are terrified about the whole idea, it provides a reassuring structure to follow. And following this may even cure them of that phobia so they'll already be looking for their next fundraising challenge.

Think product not process

One of the truly thankless tasks of any fundraiser is trying to get a charity to agree what it actually does. This very often pits departments against each other as they engage in some *Lord-of-the-Rings*-style battle for the organisation's soul, when all a fundraiser wants is a slogan.

The mission statements of many charities seem to be deliberate parodies. 'The Earnest foundation is here to empower people to make informed life choices in a positive, non-discriminatory and enabling way.' Sorry, but what on earth does that mean? Even when you try to make progress, the usual response is to talk about the work carried out; for example, we run an HIV clinic, a soup kitchen, Taekwondo for under-elevens as well as a toddler group. No one talks about the end product. Why are we doing these things? For the sake of doing them? I do not think so. We do them because we want to see people gain employment, to contribute to the wider society, to make our communities safer and stronger. Charities rarely talk about this; they just talk about how they do something and not about the difference they make.

Alternatively, they get squeamish about being seen to 'take credit' for anything, because that credit should go to the charity's client/user/patient/add your own jargon. Again, it is an admirable instinct, but it makes charities look as if we are insignificant and that the client/user/patient/add your own jargon would have achieved something whether we were there or not. It is this muddled thinking that can create real problems for fundraisers in arguing for the cause. Donors want to know what would happen if the charity wasn't there and what is happening now that it is. Staff and volunteers are very often motivated by the process of doing something, but funders often just want to see what the 'product' is that they are 'buying'.

This whole terminology often jars with others within the charity. I used to run a youth centre, which has recovered sufficiently from this fact to be now truly outstanding. I picked up on the informal education jargon quite quickly, and 'process not product' became a kind of mantra. It meant that it was as important, if not more important, to look at how something was done as at what that something achieved. Were the young people involved in planning the activity or was it done unto them? What were the consequences, good and bad, of the actions involved in putting on the activity? For example, did it tackle discrimination in the way that it was done? The whole 'process not product' ideology is sound in that it acknowledges that people learn as much through the process of doing something as from the final outcome. It is therefore entirely right to say that good youth work is dependent upon a 'process not product' ideology.

'Process not product' ideology is also a very strong motivational force for many people who work within a charity. You can see this in the existential angst of those who try to articulate what the values of an organisation are. It matters terribly that things are done in a right and fair way. It is not that the final impact of these processes is incidental to them, it does still matter, but it is often the processes that motivate them to get up in the morning. Working in a charity enables them to live out the values they hold dear, and so processes really do matter.

Unfortunately, to say that good fundraising is dependent upon a 'process not product' culture is total cobblers. Funders are not motivated by how something is delivered, but by what is delivered and what impact it has. As a happy by-product, talking about products not processes also has the wonderful advantage of being brief. 'Praxis gets people back into work, enables people to overcome their addictions, provides housing for low-paid workers' and so on. Funders can have notoriously short attention spans, and their minds have often drifted before they are even half-way through many charities' mission statements. This is not to say that focusing on the product and not the process means you ignore how the money was raised. It is more that, when you communicate what your charity does, you make sure you communicate its impact first and not its means of delivery.

This separation between process and product can often mean that the whole mentality of fundraising can appear to be at odds with the dominant culture within the charity. The truth is that one culture is not better than the other. If fundraisers and funders did not focus on the product, the charity would not have the money to pay for the services it delivers. Likewise, if a charity only cared about, say, how many young people it had contact with, and not what kind of process or contact it had, the service would not be worth paying for anyway. The challenge for any charity is to acknowledge these two different cultures, for each side to respect the other and to learn how to work together.

The altruism–exchange axis

The way you fundraise should adapt according to whom you are raising money for. Certain causes lend themselves to certain ways of raising money. An obvious one is 'in-memory' fundraising with hospices. People's awareness of hospices is at an all-time high at a time of loss, and so it is natural that many would want to support them then. There is a great desire to say thank you for the care given to the loved one who has just died, and in-memory fundraising is the perfect way of doing it. This connection is fairly obvious, but there are many other examples too.

I would imagine that payroll giving would work well for charities that are involved in debt advice or poverty. Gaining the support of a healthcare provider to sponsor your health programme in Central America would be similarly successful. Having a water company or a mineral water producer sponsor digging wells in sub-Saharan Africa should also be a good tie-up. Closer to home, how about a big local employer sponsoring your job club, or a social group like the Rotary or the Lions supporting a project that arranges visits to the homes of housebound or isolated elderly people?

You need to take a step back from what you do and see the connections. It helps to think of the opposite extreme of the cause your charity is addressing. Thus, if you are tackling ill heath, what connections with health organisations are there? If you are tackling social isolation, what social groups are there? By finding a connection you immediately strengthen the tie between the supporter and the charity and that increases the chances of the relationship becoming a long-term and more generous one. It not only makes sense initially, in that it increases the positive responses to the first enquiry, but it also increases the lifetime value of those relationships, as they are more likely to stay with you. It is so much cheaper to keep an existing supporter than to recruit a new one. This should be an important factor in deciding who to approach in the first place.

One of the helpful ways of looking at your fundraising options is to consider the altruism–exchange axis. It is quite a simple idea. Take a flip chart piece of paper, turn it 'landscape' and draw an horizontal line in the middle of the sheet from left to right. Write 'altruism' at one end and 'exchange' at the other. Then plot your existing fundraising on the axis. To work out how to do that, you need to consider whether the donor is getting anything in exchange for their giving. A good 'exchange' form of fundraising is a charity shop or car boot sale. A good 'altruism' form of fundraising is the collecting box in a shop.

If you want to get a gold star, do not limit your thinking to physical things that a donor may receive back but look at the psychological too. How important is a nice thank you to the donor? Do they need that in 'exchange' for their donation? To what extent is their donation actually helping them to live out their values or their faith and as such has an 'exchange' dimension to it? If you plot all your income in this way, you see a very good snapshot picture of how you are funded; for example, map any local authority contracts too. Increasingly they now state exactly what they are getting for their grant so that they are very much at the 'exchange' end of the axis.

Legacy giving is interesting. Where would you put it on the axis? On the one hand, it must be pure altruism, because the legacy giver will receive no benefit from any donation since they will not be around to receive it. On the other hand, a surprising number of legacy donations are actually a very useful way for the person giving the legacy to sort out domestic squabbles and also to get their own back on irritating friends and relatives. If you have had your relatives bickering over who gets what from your estate when you are still alive, it must be quite tempting to wrong-foot them all by giving the whole lot to a charity.

As a general rule, the more popular the cause, the more the fundraising tends to be aimed towards the 'altruism' end of the axis. Put simply, when appealing to the general public, the less popular causes often have to rely on fundraising that is rewarding in itself because the cause is less likely to evoke support. The best example of this is 'charity challenge' events where people have their holidays paid for by their friends' donations. Oops, sorry, I mean where they sacrificially give up their holidays in order to endure physical and mental torment in the interests of eliciting donations for a cause they value. In these instances, it is the means of fundraising that often encourages donations as much as the cause. People give because they want to reward the bravery or endeavour of the person concerned, as much as they want to give to a certain cause. As such, these forms of fundraising are very effective for causes that have less public awareness or public sympathy.

When observing your completed axis, you also need to remember that what supporters 'get back' changes from emotional through to physical things as you move from altruism to exchange. At the altruism end, they will want a kind, prompt and individualised thank-you letter so that they gain a 'warm glow' of the soul as they give the donation. At the other end, you are effectively dealing in a transaction where whatever they are receiving is worth what they are 'paying'; how the cause benefits is incidental.

By mapping your existing forms of support, you can both critique your existing practice (are you giving people what they want in return?) and also see whether it is appropriate, bearing in mind the nature of your cause. You can, as well, see whether there are ways of giving that you should be using, ways that perhaps you are not using at present. As such, this is a very useful exercise, being both practical and philosophical, and thus a really helpful holistic analysis tool.

Numbers ask questions, they don't give answers

Within a charity, the relationship between the finance people, also known as bean-counters, and the fundraisers, also known as charlatans, is often the most difficult. It is surprising how many finance people really think they could be fundraisers, which is odd, bearing in mind that the personalities needed to be successful in either discipline are diametrically opposed. I know I am biased, but I have always thought raising money was very much harder than spending it, so I suppose it is obvious which camp I am closest to. That said, the bean-counters can be very useful to fundraisers, and not just because they can give you accurate data for your snazzy presentations on your fundraising success.

Finance people can enjoy asking awkward questions about new fundraising projects; in fact, they often get an enormous kick out of it. They can sometimes see fundraisers as 'logic-light' when it comes to planning, and as a result they think fundraisers are placing the organisation under undue risk. I actually feel quite sorry for finance people sometimes, because it must be sad, however necessary it is, to be the person pointing out the flaws. To my mind, it is much more cheering to spend one's time on something rather more optimistic. I also know that the perception by some that accountants are dull and dreary can be very wide of the mark (and not just because my father was one). I think finance people can be unbelievably emotional and passionate about things – and that is one reason why they are attracted to finance, they cling to its apparent certainty like clinging to driftwood in some tempestuous sea. So while you as a fundraiser are used to chronic uncertainty – it is your constant companion – that may well not be true for them.

I am not here, though, to do some armchair psychoanalysis of finance people, though those last couple of paragraphs might suggest otherwise. This chapter is about how seriously you take their numbers. If fundraisers find it quite difficult to cope with the uncertainty and injustices of the job, imagine what finance people think about fundraising. They are desperate to reduce the odds and to guarantee fundraising success, and as such are very happy to analyse fundraising proposals in the hope that by doing this they will make the charity's future more stable and secure.

The problem with this mindset is that it forgets that fundraising is about people, who are emotional, irrational and unpredictable. Numbers are good at asking questions – How much will it raise? How much will it cost? What is the income-to-expenditure ratio and how does that compare with other possible fundraising ventures? – but they are not good at answering them. The numbers alone will not tell you whether or not something is worth doing, because people always get in the way.

Let me give you an example. I ran a fundraising campaign that was wildly successful in every regard apart from raising any money. It just about broke even. It was very clever. The 'drinks on me' campaign asked people to add on the cost of a drink to their round in the pub. That money was put in a special beer-glass-shaped collecting box and the money went to the hospice I worked for. As the patients were given a drink before lunch to stimulate their appetite, there was a direct link with the work and it helped educate the public about the hospice too (despite one person complaining that we were encouraging our patients to become alcoholics; they clearly did not understand why patients were referred to the hospice in the first place). We produced themed beer mats, posters, badges for bar staff and stickers for those who 'bought a drink'. The pubs loved it, the punters loved it, the media adored it, and it just about covered its costs.

Consequently, in finance terms, it was a poor campaign, but in reality it was one of the most successful fundraising campaigns I ran. It established new relationships with dozens and dozens of new organisations. It raised the profile of our organisation enormously. It also provided a 'hook' for the media for the capital appeal that went with it. It educated people about what we did. It broke into a totally different giving market, where the average donor was half the age of our traditional donors. You can't tell all of this from a spreadsheet.

That is not to say that questions should not be asked, just that sometimes the answers are as complicated and complex as are the reasons for giving. The numbers will not provide a definitive answer on whether or not something works or whether or not something should proceed. They will ask lots of good questions, but they cannot be the casting vote.

I think it is the complexity of the reasons behind giving that explains why really good fundraisers have such an uncannily accurate gut instinct. On some level, deep down in the subconscious, they can actually see that this campaign will be successful and why, but do not have the 'logic speak' to reassure people as to the reason.

I went on one of those psychological profiling courses a few years ago. I found the whole thing an absolute hoot, as my personality type would apparently. I personally couldn't think of a better way of spending a day than thinking and talking about me and, as I never take myself vaguely seriously, I was very happy to be critiqued. One of the things that my personality type is good at is 'making a compelling argument for whatever they want'. I roared with laughter on reading that, because I knew it was true. We are still, as a society, preoccupied with thinking that the winning of an argument establishes truth. The reality, as any good arguer will tell you, is that very often this is total rubbish. I can find compelling reasons for any old load of fundraising cobblers.

Logical debate is not the best way of identifying fundraising success. A better way, by far, is to be 'out there' with your antennae twitching. If you are good at reading people and you spend a lot of time with those who support your cause, your ideas will be shaped by what you know will work. Your supporters will not only show you which ideas to pursue but also how to pursue them and how to communicate them. Numbers are good at checking that your antennae are still functioning properly, but they should never replace the antennae themselves. Besides, if they did, it would really hurt.

Giving is good for you

There is a motivation in fundraising that is rarely mentioned, like an embarrassing relative at a family reunion. It is a motivation for giving that just seems too wrong and takes us into ambivalent moral territory. What is this hideous offence against all right-minded fundraisers? Well, whisper it quietly, but it is this: giving is good for you. Not only is it good for the beneficiaries of the charity but it is actually rather good for those who give too. In fact, it is so good for givers that it would be worth them doing, even if their gift did not make any difference to anyone with whom the charity works. Maybe their donation did get spent on that futile, poorly thought-through project, which put the work of the wider charity back ten years due to the disastrous execution of a misguided plan. But at least the act of giving did the giver some good.

Giving to a charity so that you will benefit just feels wrong. However, there are many benefits of giving to charity which in themselves are things you would want to purchase if you could. 'Buying' a donation is a perfect little treat for yourself because, for one little gift-aided donation, you get that marvellous little essential for mental health – perspective.

You could argue we are as egocentric a society as you could possibly imagine. Everything is me, me, me. It is all about how I feel, how much I earn, how big my house is, what kind of car I have and where I go on holiday. Me, me, me. Our lives are all about fulfilling our wishes, our hopes and our needs. Many of us go along to therapy so that we can spend a whole uninterrupted hour talking about ourselves. Frankly, after a while, it becomes somewhat tedious. The more we think about ourselves, the more important we think we are. And the more important we think we are, the more we think about ourselves. It is a vicious circle. We become ever more self-absorbed, our one and only reference point for anything is 'how will this affect me?' To put it bluntly, we become pretty tiresome.

For that reason, we need something to shake us out of our self-centred lives, and giving to charity does that. We realise that, if our 'stressful' big decision is whether to accept a new job or stick with our old one with a big pay rise, that pales into insignificance compared with having to decide which members of your family get fed today. As a society, we have, to state the obvious, so much to be thankful for. By and large those who give to charities are those who have done rather well out of the society in which they live. It is easy to forget that many, many people do not thrive in the way that we do. By giving to charity we are looking at others rather than ourselves. That sense of perspective makes our own difficulties more manageable. As Professor David Myers put it, 'happiness is less a matter of getting what we want than of wanting what we have.' Giving can give you this perspective.

Another benefit of giving is that it enables us to deliver something of our personal manifesto. Warm words are easy, doing something about injustice, suffering, poverty or whatever is altogether harder. Giving to charity enables you to do that. One of the things I really struggle with is the way we do Christmas in this country. I am no fan of twinkly religion or rampant commercialism, and Christmas in my humble opinion can often be both. Imagine the joy and delight when Oxfam (and others) came up with the truly brilliant idea of enabling people to buy presents for people who actually need them rather than for those who neither need them nor, in truth, often want them either. I think there is no debate between buying unwanted and un-needed presents and stopping someone from dying of a preventable disease. I appreciate this makes me a bit bah-humbugish in some people's eyes, but I can live with that. *Oxfam unwrapped* enabled me to live out that bit of my personal manifesto on converting Christmas. Just think of it: it could be the one day of the year when, rather than indulge ourselves yet further, we, as a society, spend a day focusing on those who have so much less than we do. It could be fantastic. It would give Christmas more moral credibility; it would also (as a nice by-product) come some way closer to the original Christmas story. At its most basic, because I did not send my relatives presents they did not want, fewer people will die and suffer. Sounds like a good Christmas message to me.

Hence, I think giving is great. It reminds me of what I have and what I take for granted, and it lets me tackle some of the injustices I feel most strongly about. Of course, there is a danger here, because isn't the second reason giving is good for you (living out my manifesto) actually working against the first (perspective)? Possibly. And even if not, isn't there a danger this is just another example of a self-obsessed Westerner who manages to turn even helping with the alleviation of the suffering of others into some gigantic ego trip about themselves and how marvellous they are? I suppose it could be seen as that. It seems to me, though, that this is an unavoidable part of the fundraiser's message. You cannot avoid the impact on the giver, or if you do, you miss a trick. At the same time, if the message is not primarily about, and driven by, the injustice and suffering, you will not get the perspective. I would argue you do need both. The world is not about you, that is true, but that does not mean you do not exist or have no significance. Indeed, you have a great responsibility and that is what giving can show you.

'I don't care about the money; I just want to be wonderful'

Good fundraisers contribute to organisations in many different ways. One of the unexpected ways they contribute is by often being the scapegoat for all the ills within the charity. Their roles are scrutinised in a way that other professions are not, their motives are questioned far more than of those with other roles and their (in)competence is judged far more than that of others within the organisation. Why is this?

As with most things in life, the answer is complex. All of the following contribute to the general suspicion and disdain that so many fundraisers can experience:

Money is bad

Many people who work in charities believe this basic principle (apart from their own salaries, of course). 'The love of money is the root of all evil', 1 Timothy 6:10 (a mis-translation, by the way, it is actually closer to 'money is the root of all kinds of evil', which is similar but not exactly the same, although it is an argument that is probably not worth pursuing now). Money gets people into debt, money is taken away from the unemployed and lack of money denies choice, education, health and happiness. Money breeds division, suffering and despair. If your stock-in-trade is filthy lucre, you are not going to be popular.

Rights, not handouts

The beneficiaries of the charity (a term that will appal many people who work for charities) should not have to beg for money via fundraisers; they should be given it 'through taxation'. This is rarely if ever squared with the reality that if a political party wants to lose, it will say it will increase taxes. It is seen as immoral for people to have their basic needs met through the whims of the rich and powerful who may, of course, spend their money on a yacht instead.

Shallow end

Charity workers are a diving pool, fundraisers a paddling pool. Fundraisers focus on the superficial, vain and shallow, and are motivated and focused on yukky money while charity workers are motivated by kindness, compassion, justice and love.

Thus fundraisers have different values and motivations, and their role only exists because of the cruel inequities in society. Seen in this light, the friction between non-fundraisers and fundraisers is not too remarkable. It is for these reasons and others that a senior fundraiser, when I asked her whether she encouraged her fundraising staff to mix with other charity staff, exclaimed 'Good God, no!' She described herself as a 'firewall' between her staff and others within the organisation. It is not that surprising that fundraisers suffer from stress. Despised from within and often reviled from without, fundraisers are inclined to cling together just to stay sane.

The truth is that fundraisers inhabit a murky moral world because charities do too. Ever since the welfare state, the role of charities has been somewhat fuzzy. Should there be charities or should there not? Didn't the welfare state kind of do away with the need for charities? Weren't handouts replaced with rights? If the public sector is 'statutory', does that mean charities are 'optional'? It is all a tangled mess, and fundraisers can often be placed at the sharp end. I do believe that fundraising charities are one of the better models for bringing about a more just world. But many do not, and many just instinctively do not like the idea but have not thought about why they don't.

In trying to resolve tensions between fundraisers and non-fundraisers, I have often had to take everyone back to the basics of what the organisation is and what it is for. If a charity did not receive donations, how would it survive? There are only two other options that I can see. The first is to be funded directly through taxation. The problem with that is a) people do not like paying taxes and so there is never enough taxation money around, and b) taxation ceases to be perceived as 'our money' and becomes the government's money and thus people may find it easier to waste it.

Therefore, if it does not come from individuals and it does not come from the government, where can it come from? Nowhere. Let's just not need it in the first place. We can all give our time for free, we'll grow our own resources, make our own buildings, clean ourselves in the river and so on. This is all nonsense, of course, but I am amazed how often I see this view expressed in more impressive-sounding terms. Fundraising acknowledges the reality of the Western world, which is that money is often needed for care and compassion. Fluffy-bunny sentimentality does not pay rates, rent, heat, light, wages, equipment, resources and the like. If you want to show you care, you hand money over. Some may not like this reality, but that does not mean it is untrue. Marilyn Monroe said: 'I don't care about the money; I just want to be wonderful.' It is an opinion that I suspect a multi-millionaire might find easier to hold. The reality for charities is that, to be wonderful, they must care about money, because they need money in order to be wonderful.

Fundraising should not be carried out solely due to pragmatism, the 'necessary evil' argument. What is often perceived as a negative about fundraising can be seen as a positive if seen from a different angle. For example, take the argument about rights, not handouts. By asking people for money for a cause, a fundraiser is forming a bridge between the organisation and the community it works within (volunteers do a similar thing). If money drops from the skies, the impetus to engage with a community is lost (have a look at a charity that receives most of its donations from legacies and you often see the same thing; they are not accountable to anyone for how they spend the money so it is easier, and more of a possibility, that they cease to engage with the communities they work within).

Fundraisers say to their charity: why are we doing this? Why is it important? What difference is it making? They challenge the charity to spend money wisely, to ensure the charity is getting the biggest 'bang' for every 'buck' they receive. I can still vividly remember someone handing me a cheque for the charity I worked for. It was their inheritance that they had just received. They were not by any means rich, not unless delivering milk pays much more than I think it does. They lived humbly and simply. But did they sacrifice their own wishes, dreams and desires so that others would not suffer? You bet they did. That holiday, that new car, paying off the mortgage: we can all find ways of spending money. They did not do any of those things because they wanted more for others to have it. When you see that level of sacrificial generosity, you make quite sure you do not waste a penny of it. It is a fantastic financial discipline.

Creativity in mysterious places

I have often gone to conferences in search of enlightenment for my fundraising challenges, to hear of a new approach, theory or insight that will transform my practice. I have frequently left with a bad taste in my mouth, and not just because of the terrible coffee. I would look around me wondering whether I was the only one who didn't get it, who left more baffled and confused than they arrived. These sessions often made fundraising seem so terribly complicated, when, to me, it has always been a straightforward if difficult challenge. In the past, I used to use a six-word Calvin & Hobbes cartoon to illustrate the challenge of raising money. Calvin, a six-year-old boy asks his stuffed tiger friend Hobbes (who comes to life in his imagination) 'do you have any money?' to which Hobbes replied 'nope'. We can dress it up in all manner of ways, but fundraising really is that simple – we need money for some charitable cause, money we do not have.

It is the prosaic nature of the challenge which can lead us to think prosaically too. Our creativity gets dulled through the repetitive nature of the task, and we struggle to break out of well-established patterns of behaviour. One of the ways we can be rescued from this scenario is by animals on the underground.

Paul Middlewick, a designer based in London, first discovered them in the 1980s. He worked out that, if you highlight some lines on the London underground map, you can draw the outline shape of an animal. He first spotted an elephant, and the rest, as they say, is history. Fish, dogs, whales, parrots and many more soon followed. The joy was in looking at something functional in a completely different way and seeing things that you hadn't seen before.

As such, this is a great creative exercise when we need to reimagine ways of doing things. The lines of the map are as familiar to most of us as the resources and talents we have at our disposal for our fundraising activities. What is different is imagining them in a completely different way, creating something entirely unexpected through using what we have in a radically different way.

When I have asked groups to find and draw animals on the underground map, it has always led to fascinating conversations and insights. For some, this takes them way, way outside their comfort zone. They look at a series of lines on a piece of paper and see… lines. They really struggle to see patterns or shapes. This is one of the reasons it has to be done as a small group exercise, or at least in pairs, because otherwise it really might not get very far.

Others see this as the most effortless and enjoyable activity, and never want it to stop. Once they have seen one, they see dozens. You can almost feel the brain fizzing as they look at an incredibly familiar thing in a completely new way.

There's normally a third group, too, who are 'completer finishers'. They might not see the initial outline but can add the finishing touches with real flair to make the animal unique.

The surprising thing to me is that you can never really work out which group people will fit into. People who would not consider themselves 'arty', and who other people would definitely not consider 'arty', find they have a natural flair for it. So in the exercise we learn more about each other but also start to see each other in a different light, with skills and insights which we may not have fully appreciated before.

Of course, there are many activities like this which achieve similar ends. The point here is to stress the need for activities like this to reframe the challenges we face and what we can bring to meet those challenges. Such activities also enable us to see each other in a different way, and so discover new ways for how we can work together as a team. Exercises like this can help us reset our fundraising plans, unlocking creativity we did not know we had and enabling us to see new opportunities. It's the perfect antidote to 'same old' fundraising.

The exercise reminds me of a favourite quote from Mary Karr, the American poet, essayist and memoirist, 'I always start off thinking I know what is important, and it's never what's important, it's always something else… I think you get ambushed by the truth.' I love the notion of being ambushed by the truth, and sometimes we particularly need that. If we follow the same paths, and do the same things, we get what we always have got. But if we start off intentionally to go in a different path, to try a different way, to stimulate the under-exercised parts of our brain, we raise the possibility of being ambushed by the truth, and who doesn't want that?

Sanctified by use: can money be laundered?

Fundraising is at times a moral swamp and working your way through it can be a difficult and challenging experience. William Booth, founder of the Salvation Army, was asked about the acceptance of 'tainted money', and his conclusion was 't'aint enough of it'. He certainly seemed to believe that money was amoral, and it is how you used it that mattered. Fundraising is caught right in the midst of this ethical dilemma. Within the charity sector, money is often seen in negative terms, which is ironic as I would say our entire society is geared around acquiring it. Where money comes from and how we use it are therefore very important fundraising dilemmas.

If you want to start an argument, ask people who work with or support your charity who the charity should accept money from. If you work for a health charity, should you accept a donation from a tobacco company? If you work for a youth charity, should you take money from someone suspected of being a drug dealer? Should you ever take money from companies that make armaments? Should a religious organisation take money from the National Lottery? On one thing I can be absolutely sure: you will never get agreement on these kinds of questions. However, by asking the questions publicly, you will be showing people that there is no right answer and, therefore, that the dilemmas you face are very difficult to resolve.

It is enormously important that you ask these questions before you start your fundraising. There is little more frustrating than spending an age developing a sponsorship agreement with a local firm only for it to be pulled at the eleventh hour because a trustee did not want the charity to be associated with that company, for whatever reason. These kinds of decisions are quite rightly the responsibility of the trustees, but you cannot keep going to them asking them about specific individuals or organisations, so you need some broad guidance.

How do you go about gaining that broad guidance? You need to tackle the following issues head on. First, is it different if the donation is a public one? If you work for a cancer charity and a tobacco company wants to give you £100,000, does it make a difference if it is to be publicised or not? This links to another question which you also need to answer: do you believe that by taking a donation you are endorsing the way that money was acquired by the individual or organisation concerned? To carry on with the hypothesis of a cancer charity (because it is an extreme case, and so a bit easier to see with some clarity), is the £100,000 effectively assuaging the conscience of a guilty company and therefore (in the company's eyes) justifying them in continuing with their damaging trade, or is it taking £100,000 from a tobacco company and using it for a good purpose – money that would otherwise just be reinvested to encourage yet more people to be smokers? The honest answer to both questions is 'probably, yes'. Within this is the dilemma. How much can a charity control and how much can it not control? Is it really the responsibility of a charity to attempt to dictate the way another organisation or individual works, or is that their responsibility?

There is a real danger with this issue that a charity can become more concerned with being seen to be morally right but bankrupt in preference to morally dubious but doing the job it was created to do. A charity's responsibility is to its beneficiaries, and if a donation is turned down, and thus the work with the beneficiaries reduced, there has to be a compelling reason for it. The counter-argument is that if a donation from a morally dubious source is made public, other donors will stop giving in protest so that the cumulative effect of accepting the dodgy donation is to end up with less money. This is obviously linked to whether the donation will be publicised or not, but, even if there is no agreement to publicise it, it may well become public knowledge. Therefore, it is very important that any such donations are fully debated before being accepted and that representatives of the charity know what to say if challenged publicly about such gifts.

Part of your job as a fundraiser when dealing with this issue is to ensure that all involved in the charity realise how difficult this kind of decision is. If the donation should become public, people should not be forced to say they agree with something that they do not agree with but, equally, they should not criticise the charity in public for the decision it has made. It is important that all involved accept that the decision is difficult and that they abide by the decision made following a full and open debate.

There is yet another angle on this, which is important and deepens the moral swamp yet further. There is an argument that accepting a donation establishes an educational opportunity for the charity with the individual or organisation concerned. Thus, by accepting a donation, you create an opportunity to educate and inform an organisation so that it will then choose to change its harmful practice. If you did not accept this donation, and so did not have this relationship with the organisation, you would not have the opportunity to persuade it to change its practice. Lobbying the organisation 'from the outside' would not be as effective as 'educating from within'. Of course, the educating and persuading might not work, but if you did not accept the donation, you wouldn't have had the chance that it might.

When at St Luke's Hospice, I really wanted to do a PR campaign on the nature of the work. The public perception was that it was a place where people went to die. Of course, it was in many cases, but it was also about becoming involved in supporting and caring for people who still very much had a life to be lived, even after the terminal diagnosis. I put forward the argument, which I lost, that any communication if it is to be effective must form a bridge between the organisation and the individual. We must establish some common understanding. Therefore, we would start our PR campaign by acknowledging that we do indeed care for the dying, and that we would acknowledge this by using images of a graveyard on our posters.

The medics were not convinced, surprisingly enough, but I think my logic was right even if my political sensitivities were not. When you start working with someone, you simply have to form a meeting place of the mind, otherwise you will never meet. Similarly, you have to see a donation as an educational opportunity. People should not be expected to sign up to all of your values before making a donation, nor to understand fully the reasons why they should change their practices (if they should) before you have even sent one thank-you letter. One of the hospice supporters, a prominent local businessman, told me he supported the hospice because then he did not feel so guilty about smoking cigars; it was almost a kind of insurance policy. The morality may be confused, and I might not agree with it, but it seems absurd to reject his donation and the possibility to change that behaviour just because I do not share his opinion.

So what do I really think? In truth, I think it is extremely rare that there are sufficient grounds for rejecting a donation. Even if a donation is made public and even if it comes from what may be perceived as a morally dubious source. I believe it is the charity's responsibility to argue its case. Moral issues are not black and white, there is no right or wrong, so the impact on the public is very much dictated by the skills of the charity in communicating its decision and the rationale behind it. Often a charity panics in these situations and issues a 'no comment' at best. That is worse than useless in that a charity is seen to have no defence to any accusations made against it. The charity needs to explain why it made the decision and acknowledge how difficult it was, and how many valid opinions there are which cannot be reconciled with each other. Once that has been done, there is only one key thing it must do, and that is not to back down. Once a decision has been made, you must stick to it. If you do not, it just makes you look weak and indecisive.

The five essential truths

Fundraising is not an easy business. The tasks themselves are relatively simple, but the ambivalence over money, both within your organisation and in society, can mean that you feel as if you are wading through particularly viscous treacle.

If your working role is one that does not excite others, it is very important that you can excite yourself about it. You need to be able to motivate yourself and to be able to cope with the difficulties and frustrations that it brings. You also need to have a pretty mature understanding of your limitations, and indeed the limitations of others, if you are to enjoy and prosper in this weird business.

I am not sure if you have studied male initiation ceremonies – there are not many who have – but a very wise person called Richard Rohr has. In his book *Adam's Return*, he argues the case that young men have not been taught the five essential truths, because we have done away with the initiation ceremonies that taught them. It is a fascinating read if you are interested in such things, but in case you are not, I will let you in on what the five essential truths are. I think these apply to us all, and I would recommend that you write them on a piece of paper and stick it where you will see it regularly. If you do, mental well-being should not be far behind. The five truths are:

- life is hard
- you are not that important

- your life is not about you
- you are not in control
- you are going to die

It is not the cheeriest list of truths to keep as a constant reminder. However, if you understand and accept them, the inevitable frustrations that you feel will be easier to manage. Let's go through them one by one.

Life is hard

Fundraising is not easy. It is a difficult task. It is concerned with asking people to do something they often do not want to do. They may well want to spend their money on themselves not on someone else, so they often won't like you very much for trying to persuade them to do something they do not want to do. If you are finding fundraising hard work, you are probably on the right lines because it was never meant to be easy nor was it claimed to be. There is no magic fundraising formula that makes the money just pour in so that you spend all day writing thank-you letters. That does not happen; life is hard, so do not beat yourself up over it not being easy. It is not meant to be.

You are not that important

Your job is fairly straightforward and simple; the givers are the people who are doing something extraordinary. Of course, you are important; someone is needed to ask and manage the giving, but you are not *that* important. Lighten up. When things are going well, do not take all the credit, because then you will have some moral consistency when you do not take all the blame on those occasions when things may go wrong. Accept that you have a role and that you are important but that you are not *that* important. Believe me, when you do, it is wonderfully liberating.

Your life is not about you

All good fundraisers constantly deflect praise on to their colleagues. It should not be about your name in the paper or putting yourself forward for meaningless awards; it should be about others. You should do this because it is the right thing to do and because you raise more money by doing it. Also, the focus of your work should always, always, always be the beneficiaries of your charity. Fundraising is a mechanism for giving deserving causes what they have a right to receive. It is those causes that should motivate you, and it is those causes that everyone remembers when you have sat down after giving a talk or after they have read your article.

You are not in control

Stop making ludicrous claims of influence that you know, deep down, you cannot support. All the credit for any money you raise goes to the ones who give it. Fundraising is about lessening the odds, not guaranteeing success. It takes bravery to say this. People want to know that someone out there is in control so that they can stop worrying. It might be an unpopular thing to say, but you need to say it: the control rests with the funders. Your cause will always be dependent on them, and that is actually a good thing, if uncomfortable as well. A badly run fundraising event in sunshine raises more money than a well-run fundraising event in the rain. It is not fair, but it is true, so get over it and move on.

You are going to die

How soon will largely depend on how well you cope with the stress of raising money. Death is the one thing that we all have in common. So do not waste your time. Make sure what you do is good, be committed to it, work hard and be absolutely focused on making sure that something is achieved at the end. Do not get wrapped up in any petty, personality-driven feuds; just focus on making a difference.

The five essential truths are a must for your own mental health when it comes to fundraising. There is another very important piece of advice too: know thyself, and know when to get the hell out of there. There is a limit to what you can do, and you need to realise that sometimes there is simply nothing you can do to make things right. You just have to leave. Fundraising is only a small piece of a complicated jigsaw that makes a strong charity. You cannot control many things that are necessary for fundraising success. Don't beat yourself up about this either, just accept it as an inevitability and realise that every job has its natural shelf life.

> *I trace the rainbow through the rain,*
> *And feel the promise is not vain,*
> *That morn shall tearless be.*
>
> George Matheson

Never cease exploring

Greg LeMond was a professional cyclist in the 1980s. He was asked whether training gets easier the fitter you get. 'It never gets easier, you just go faster', he replied. There's so much truth in that. I can't say that I have found fundraising has got easier the more I have learned, or practised. But that practice enables you to learn more about yourself and fundraising and, as a result, get better at it.

It can be easy to think that when we become brilliant at something, we can then avoid hard work – it will become effortless. Not sure I have even fleetingly been a brilliant fundraiser, but it has certainly always been hard work. There are also dangers in thinking the inverse is true, that if we find fundraising to be hard work, then we can't be brilliant. Fundraising is a confidence game, and letting thoughts like that worm their way into your psyche can really hurt your ability to *be* brilliant. So Greg LeMond's quote is for us all, to remind us that we should expect things to be hard, but we also should expect to get better at things the more we practise – as long as we practise well.

The practising well is key. As a child, I spent easily as much time playing football as David Beckham, yet somehow he became a global footballing icon and I never progressed from some nifty goals with a tennis ball in the alley down the back of our house. Was it all due to lack of talent? Well, I think, that was part of the answer, but Matthew Syed's book

Bounce that I mention earlier in this book offers a more plausible explanation. He says that one of the noticeable things about elite sports people, compared to those who hoof a tennis ball in an alleyway, is that they practise what they cannot do rather what they can. He calls this 'purposeful practice', the striving for something that is currently just out of reach. A hallmark of success is the willingness to forego the pleasure of executing over and over again what we know and do well, for the pain of trying and failing over and over again to do something new until we succeed. As Van Gogh put it, 'I keep on making *what I can't do yet*, in order to learn to be able to do it'.

This commitment to grow and to learn is true for everything, I guess, and so fundraising is no exception. It is also the case for organisations as much as for individuals – how much resource are we expending to develop and grow as opposed to repeat what has worked before?

This isn't just about money and time; in fact, it is mainly *not* about money and time but about mindset. Do we welcome and encourage innovation, which is inherently more risky? Do we practise what we cannot do as much as what we can? If I can sneak in a Machiavelli quote here, 'there is nothing more difficult to carry out, nor more doubtful of success, nor more dangerous to handle, than to initiate a new order of things.' It's hard to innovate, yet it is essential to us as individuals and organisations, and so must be something we value and encourage within our fundraising practice.

It is essential that we never cease exploring if we wish to be successful in fundraising. When we do, it often takes us back to where we first were, but, as T. S. Eliot wrote in *The Four Quartets*, we truly know it in a way we never knew before.

As we successfully innovate, we really arrive back where our charities first started, back to that time when what was needed and what worked drove our thinking and being – not what we had always done. We're focusing back on the primary purpose, not the means we've used to deliver it in the past. So the innovation and exploration helps us to arrive where we started – what is the best way for us to be asking people to give? – but our experience enables us to know it in a way we never knew before.

A final thought. Of course, fundraising is not really about money at all. A theological understanding of the word 'charity' is 'unlimited love and kindness'. I truly adore this understanding of the word. It is not so much an organisational status, or benevolence, but a human desire to care for others with unlimited love and kindness. That is what fundraising enables and brings about. As far as human endeavours go, that's a pretty wonderful use of our time.

References and notes

Page vii – Oscar Wilde, *An Ideal Husband*, London, A&C Black, 1996, p.17, lines 162–3.

Page 9 – '50 things to do before you're 11¾' [web page], National Trust, www.nationaltrust.org.uk/visit/50-things, accessed 7 March 2024.

Page 20 – Miranda Sawyer, 'Something of the nighy' [web article], *The Guardian*, www.theguardian.com/film/2004/oct/31/1, 31 October 2004. Courtesy of Guardian News & Media Ltd.

Page 26 – George Matheson, 'O love that wilt not let me go', The Scottish Hymnal, Edinburgh, T. Nelson and Sons, 1885, p. 221.

Page 27 – Nanci Griffith, 'If wishes were changes', Flyer, 1994.

Page 27 – Charlotte Higgins, *Under Another Sky: Journeys in Roman Britain*, London, Vintage, 2014.

Page 28 – Charlotte Higgins, 'How to decode an ancient Roman's handwriting' [web article], *The New Yorker*, www.newyorker.com/tech/annals-of-technology/how-to-decode-an-ancient-romans-handwriting, 1 May 2017.

Page 44 – Walter Isaacson, *Einstein. His life and universe*, New York, Simon & Schuster, 2007, notes, 'Letter from Einstein to son on February 5, 1930'.

Page 50 – Gerry Goffin and Carole King, 'You Make Me Feel (Like a Natural Woman)', 1967, originally sung by Aretha Franklin. Copyright © Sony Music Publishing UK Ltd.

Page 56 – Kate Fox, *Watching the English: The Hidden Rules of English Behaviour*, London, Hodder and Stoughton, 2005.

Page 59 – What General John Sedgwick actually said is 'they couldn't hit an elephant from this distance', but I have taken the liberty of re-ordering the phrase because it is funnier. Martin McMahon, 'The Death of General John Sedgwick' [web page], Sedgwick Genealogy North America, www.sedgwick.org/na/families/robert1613/B/2/9/2/B292-sedgwick-gen-john-death.html, accessed 7 March 2024.

Page 63 – Chris Hadfield, *An Astronaut's Guide to Life on Earth*, London, Macmillan, 2013.

Page 63 – The original quote goes 'A map *is not* the territory it represents, but, if correct, it has a *similar structure* to the territory, which accounts to its usefulness'; Alfred Korzybski, *Science and Sanity: An introduction to non-Aristotelian systems and general semantics*, Lancaster, Pennsylvania, The International Non-Aristotelian Library Publishing Company, 1933, p. 58.

Page 64 – Chris Hadfield, *An Astronaut's Guide to Life on Earth*, London, Macmillan, 2013, p. 71.

Page 64 – Ibid., p. 41.

Page 65 – Ibid., p. 192.

Page 68 – 'Lawn-Chair Pilot Faces $4,000 in Fines' [web article], *The New York Times*, www.nytimes.com/1982/12/19/us/lawn-chair-pilot-faces-4000-in-fines.html, 19 December 1982.

Page 69 – 'Truck Driver Takes to Skies in a Lawn Chair' [web article], *The New York Times*, www.nytimes.com/1982/07/03/us/truck-driver-takes-to-skies-in-a-lawn-chair.html, 3 July 1982.

Page 69 – Ron Rose, 'Keep dreaming', [web article], Arlington Today, https://web.archive.org/web/20131019194733/http:/www.arlingtontoday.com/keep-dreaming-cms-187, 29 May 2013.

Page 74 – Frank Furedi, *Culture of Fear. Risk-taking and the morality of low expectation*, London, Continuum, 2002, p. 13.

Page 75 – Ralph Waldo Emerson, 'Emerson Selected Journals 1841–1877 Vol. 2' [web page], A Raeder's Journal, www.doyletics.com/arj/rwe2jour.shtml, accessed 7 March 2024.

Page 83 – See Marie Jahoda, 'Work, employment, and unemployment: Values, theories, and approaches in social research', *American Psychologist*, 36, 1981, pp. 184–191; Marie Jahoda, *Employment and unemployment: A social-psychological analysis*, Cambridge, England, Cambridge University Press, 1982; Marie Jahoda, 'Manifest and latent functions' in *The Blackwell Encyclopedic Dictionary of Organizational Behaviour*, edited by Nigel Nicholson, Oxford, England, Blackwell, 1998, pp. 317–18.

Page 90 – 'Address before the Wisconsin State Agricultural Society. Milwaukee, Wisconsin, 30 September 1859' [web page], Abraham Lincoln Online, www.abrahamlincolnonline.org/lincoln/speeches/fair.htm, accessed 7 March 2024.

Page 91 – Matthew Syed, *Bounce: The myth of talent and the power of practice*, London, HarperCollins Publishers, 2011.

Page 104 – See Daniel Goleman, *Emotional Intelligence: Why it can matter more than IQ*, New York, Bantam Books, 1995.

Page 117 – Roald Dahl, *Going Solo*, London, Jonathan Cape, 1986.

Page 123 – Richard Rodgers and Oscar Hammerstein II, 'Do-Re-Mi', *The Sound of Music*, 1959.

Page 139 – David Myers, *Does Economic Growth Improve Public Morale* [PDF] *Enough!*, 1997, https://pub-fb5027e0bdfb4fc4ab71242ed2116543.r2.dev/uploads/Does-Economic-Growth-Improve-Human-Morale.pdf, p. 3, accessed 7 March 2024.

Page 144 – 'Marilyn Monroe Quote' [web page], LibQuotes, https://libquotes.com/marilyn-monroe/quote/lbm3m4c, accessed 7 March 2024.

Page 146 – 'Calvin and Hobbes by Bill Watterson for June 27, 1987' [web page], GoComics, www.gocomics.com/calvinandhobbes/1987/06/27#, accessed 7 March 2024.

Page 146 – See https://animalsontheunderground.com for more information.

Page 148 – Gaby Wood, 'Exactly as she remembers it' [web article], *The Guardian*, www.theguardian.com/books/2001/jun/24/biography.features, 24 June 2001. Courtesy of Guardian News & Media Ltd.

Page 149 – Beth Breeze, 'Should charities accept contrition cash from dubious donors?' [web article], *The Guardian*, www.theguardian.com/voluntary-sector-network/2017/nov/24/charities-contrition-cash-rich-dubious-donors-harvey-weinstein, 24 November 2017. Courtesy of Guardian News & Media Ltd.

Page 154 – Richard Rohr, *Adam's Return. The five promises of male initiation*, New York, The Crossroad Publishing Company, 2021.

Page 157 – George Matheson, 'O love that wilt not let me go', The Scottish Hymnal, Edinburgh, T. Nelson and Sons, 1885, p. 221.

Page 158 – Greg LeMond and Mark Hom, *The Science of Fitness: Power, performance, and endurance*, Cambridge, Massachusetts, Academic Press, 2014, p. 122.

Page 159 – Mathew Syed, *Bounce. The myth of talent and the power of practice*, London, HarperCollins Publishers, 2011.

Page 159 – 'To Anthon van Rappard. Neuen, on or about Tuesday, 18 August 1885' [web page], Vincent van Gogh. The Letters, https://vangoghletters.org/vg/letters/let528/letter.html, accessed 7 March 2024.

Page 159 – Nicollò Machiavelli, 'The Prince' [web page], The Project Gutenberg, www.gutenberg.org/cache/epub/57037/pg57037-images.html, accessed 7 March 2024.

Page 159 – T.S. Eliot, 'Little Gidding', *The Four Quartets*, London, Faber and Faber, 1944.